Praise for *How to Build a Social Media Community for Your Nonprofit in 90 Days*

"Social media is a journey through peaks and valleys and winding yellow brick roads, where you ultimately hope to discover the powerful voice you inherently possess. This book is the only map you'll need. And Julia is the only guide you'll need. She will help you discover clarity in your purpose, captivate and grow your supporter base, and finally, cultivate long-lasting relationships using social media."

–John Haydon, Author of *Facebook Marketing for Dummies, Facebook Marketing All-In-One*, and the much anticipated *DonorCARE*

"With clarity, wisdom and wit, Julia Campbell has crafted an essential resource for every nonprofit. She takes the mystery and stress out of social media and offers us a clear, easy-to-follow roadmap to building an engaged community. Don't just read this book, put it into practice!"

–Rod Arnold, Founder of Leading Good.
CMO of Soles4Souls. Former COO of charity: water

"Julia's book captures her practical, no-nonsense approach to social media. With empathy that speaks to her vast experience with nonprofits, Julia has provided an easy guide to navigate social media and help nonprofits find their authentic voice."

–Mona Raina, Director of
New Services Development, TechSoup

How to Build and Mobilize A
Social Media Community
for Your Nonprofit in
90 DAYS

JULIA CAMPBELL

BOLD & BRIGHT
—— M E D I A ——

Published by Bold & Bright Media, LLC.
319 Becks Church Road
Lexington, North Carolina 27292
Boldandbrightmedia.com

ISBN-13: 978-0-692-86712-9

Library of Congress Control Number: 2020931814

Bold & Bright Media is a multimedia publishing company committed to bold hearts, bright minds, and storytellers whose experiences will inspire and compel others to grow in their own greatness. For more information visit BoldandBrightMedia.com.

Dedication

This book is dedicated to my friend and mentor, the brilliant, hilarious, courageous, and inimitable John Haydon, without whom I would have never started down this path.

Contents

The promise: After completing 90 days of activities, you will walk away with a tactical and actionable Nonprofit Social Media Blueprint and Social Media Calendar. These documents will help you to reach the right people, inspire them to participate in your work and spread your message, and create real results for your nonprofit on social media. For additional tools visit www.jcsocialmarketing.com/socialmediabook.

Part Two: CAPTIVATE

Foreword
By Beth Kanter

In 2003, almost a decade since the birth of the world wide web, the age of social media was born. Dubbed Web 2.0, it marked a shift from one-to-many broadcast type digital communication to real person-to-person engagement. The Social Media Age started with blogs, where the commenting and community were just as important as the content.

Then a Harvard University student named Mark Zukerberg launched a social network for students—what we know as Facebook—and everything changed. In 2007, Facebook started to scale by making it available for everyone, not just college students, with a bold, audacious goal of connecting the entire world. A few years later, Facebook introduced brand pages and nonprofits started down the path of social media adoption and incorporating social media platforms like Facebook, Twitter, blogs, Instagram, and others as part of their marketing and fundraising strategies.

When I think back to the 2003 social media and nonprofit landscape, I could never have imagined how far today we have come, to today. We have witnessed the good, the bad, and the ugly impact of online social networks. From the Arab Spring to the Ice Bucket Challenge to GivingTuesday, social media has helped nonprofits scale programs, marketing, and even fundraising, due to the networked effect.

Sixteen years after the launch of Facebook, social media has entered a new phase of maturity and professionalism. In my opinion, there is no better guide to navigate successfully the next generation of social media for nonprofits than Julia Campbell and this book.

I first connected with Julia Campbell through her blogging about social media and storytelling for nonprofits many years ago. Her tips and advice were always so spot-on and practical; must-reads for nonprofits struggling to level up their social media game.

Having Julia's social media wisdom in one book with step-by-step activities will be a powerful capacity-building resource for staff of all nonprofits, whether beginners or experienced, who want to get better results with their social media. Whether your nonprofit needs help with crafting effective stories, developing the systems and skills to create and publish a regular social media editorial calendar, or platform tips that will save you time, Julia's book is filled with techniques and inspiration to keep your nonprofit going.

I have devoted over 35 years to working in, for, and with nonprofit organizations. Most of my focus has been on helping nonprofits think about digital transformation as well as the mindset changes, strategy, and innovation skills required to embrace new online technologies to support their mission-driven work. As I witnessed the birth and widespread adoption of social media, I saw that nonprofits have often faced challenges adopting new tools because it requires taking the time to acquire and internalize new skillsets. Putting a new way of working into practice can be difficult, but having the practical, time-saving tips that Julia Campbell's book offers, can make all the difference in the world.

I know how difficult it is to make the leap into effective practice with a new technology tool, especially for a small nonprofit with limited resources. In 1992, the New York Foundation for the Arts hired me to serve as the community manager and trainer for ArtsWire, an online network of arts organizations and artists. As the internet opened up the new ways for nonprofits to serve their stakeholders, I was also responsible for mastering the technology and designing and delivering trainings to nonprofits.

When I started that work, I didn't know a modem from a microwave. I was not a natural born techie. I had the passion to learn, but when I taught myself – I would often fail and it would result in hours of wasted time. What helped me was working side-by-side with a small group of geeks who generously and patiently showed me all the shortcuts and tips that made me more effective.

Julia Campbell, in this book, is giving you a gift of shoulder-to-shoulder learning and a disciplined approach to learning the tactics and skills your organization needs to master social media. If you embrace the daily practice and the tips this book offers, you will gain the confidence of knowing what works, the ability to efficiently implement a consistent social media content plan, and an actionable plan to engage your audience. You will be rewarded with improved results in fundraising, marketing, and program delivery.

Beth Kanter

Master Trainer, Speaker, & Author (www.bethkanter.org)

Books: *The Networked Nonprofit*, *Measuring the Networked Nonprofit* and *The Happy Healthy Nonprofit*.

INTRODUCTION

Imagine What's Possible

Imagine waking up each morning and being excited to get on social media, log in, and see what your nonprofit online community discussed overnight. Imagine going through the comments, the shares, the likes, the retweets, and feeling a sense of control and confidence. You know that you are influencing and inspiring people to rally around your cause. The members of your online community are excited, motivated, and engaged – they are hearing you, and even more importantly, they are listening. You are getting them to care.

You don't feel stressed or frazzled. You don't feel like you are annoying people with your posts, or pulling teeth to get them to pay attention. You don't feel smarmy, or manipulative, or yucky about the marketing messages you send out. Instead, you know in your gut that you are building something bigger than the sum of social media posts and tweets – and you can see it demonstrated in the data and analytics as well. You are focused on creating and cultivating real connections, not just simply yelling into the void and pushing out promotions to get a few more clicks.

Welcome to the new way of doing nonprofit social media.

Success in this crowded online landscape means having the confidence that you could approach your community with an ask, and they would respond. They would provide feedback. They would open their wallets. They would share your request widely with their networks. The only true currency on social media is trust and attention, and the only way to get it is through valuable communication that is craved – that people would miss if it went away.

I wrote this book to give you, and nonprofit social media managers like you, a simple, actionable, and practical framework to transform your current social media efforts in just 90 days. I know from first-hand experience that nonprofit marketers are both overwhelmed and excited by the sheer number of social media resources available to them. You've undoubtedly consumed countless blog posts, YouTube videos, webinars, online courses – all in search of some nugget of information that will help you work smarter (not harder).

As each person reading this book is unique, and because each nonprofit organization encounters distinct challenges and opportunities, you have to use your discretion and your creativity so that the activities work for *you*. It would be disingenuous and downright wrong for me to proclaim that every single nonprofit must use Twitter, or that all nonprofits adopt the Instagram Donation Sticker. There are simply no one-size-fits-all silver bullets in social media marketing.

However, I can (and I will) provide guidance and advice on the best and most effective ways to use social media for nonprofits, based on data, experience, and empirical evidence. This book will help you make educated and informed decisions about your own social media work and the ways in which your organization can fit into and adapt to the constantly changing digital world, without losing your mind.

My goal is that by the end of our time together, you will feel the confidence and clarity that come with having an actionable social media strategy that you know will move you forward – not a 20-page esoteric document that sits unread in a hard drive.

When you finish this book, and the accompanying activities, you will walk away with:

- Confidence in your knowledge of what will work—and what will not work—for your nonprofit on social media.
- The ability to focus your day and to prioritize social media tasks.
- A plan to consistently create, curate, and share compelling social media content that will resonate with your audience.
- A Nonprofit Social Media Blueprint, which will provide you with specific ways to captivate your supporters and to build a real community.

This book was written to help nonprofit social media managers:

- Better understand and make sense of the social media landscape and emerging trends that affect nonprofits.
- Feel self-assured as to where to place their focus.
- Develop a consistent strategy rather than frantically posting the week before an event or fundraising campaign.
- Turn storytelling and social media engagement into action.

One caveat. While the framework of this book is straightforward to understand and to follow, I don't want to mislead you into thinking that implementing the work during these 90 days will be a cake walk or something you can half-heartedly accomplish while streaming Netflix. Effective marketing, no matter which channels or platforms you choose, always requires curiosity, commitment, and creativity. It means getting out of your comfort zone, challenging the status quo, and actively educating others in your organization that this is work worth investing in and implementing.

Too often I hear tales of Boards that ask nonprofit marketers to whip up GoFundMe campaigns, or Facebook Fundraisers, or insert-platform-name-here accounts, to immediately fix a six-figure budget deficit. These Board members are well-meaning, sure, but they are misguided. Just because the money is out there in the universe, doesn't mean it will automatically flow to us. The internet is not an ATM. We can't continue to assume that just because we do vital, crucial work in the community that people will automatically participate – even if we ask them nicely. The truth of getting our message out there (as we know all too well) is much more complicated.

How to Build and Mobilize a Social Media Community for Your Nonprofit in 90 Days is not for the faint of heart, or for those who want a quick fix, easy fundraising hack. There are many books, courses, and consultants out there offering this kind of silver bullet, one-size-fits-all strategy to social media. We need to stop doing what everyone else is doing and disrupt social media marketing for good. As Seth Godin says, "in order to be remarkable, you have to do something worth remarking on."

The Struggle Is Real

The reality for many nonprofit social media managers on the ground is stark. You may feel like you are failing at social media, while at the same time knowing that you could and should be doing better. You may be spinning your wheels, posting and tweeting occasionally, but not getting any "results" to show for it. It's ok to think that social media is hard work, that it's an uphill battle, that it never stops and it's always on. That's the nature of the beast.

I get it. I started my nonprofit career as a one-woman marketing, development, and social media department at a small community-based nonprofit. I had to learn fundraising and nonprofit marketing on the ground, in the trenches as I went, all while wearing multiple hats and juggling way too many job responsibilities. (Sound familiar?)

No matter the size or mission of the organization, in my current consulting and coaching work, my nonprofit clients always have a handful of characteristics in common. Does this sound like you?

- Perplexed by your lack of moving the needle, when you feel like you are trying your best.

7

- Whipsawed by shiny new objects and the fast-changing pace of digital technologies.
- Unable to focus and feeling overwhelmed.
- Frustrated by the lack of buy-in or understanding at your organization.
- Held back by silos—marketing, communications, programs, etc.—and looking for more cohesion and collaboration around the social media marketing work.

I'm willing to say that *the problem is not you*. It's the way in which nonprofits approach social media and marketing in general. We starve our marketing departments, and then wonder why we are the "best kept secret in town." We tell the development/marketing person to push out uninteresting and uninspired promotions, and then we puzzle over the lack of engagement. We provide no training or resources to nonprofit social media managers, but we expect miracles from Facebook and Instagram.

How Did We Get Here?

In order to design our plan for social media success in 90 days, we have to learn from our past mistakes and truly understand why so many nonprofits struggle with getting a real return from their social media channels.

To cure the disease of bad social media marketing, we have to diagnose the symptoms – and form a strategy to combat them, one by one. What are the *real* reasons that so many nonprofits struggle to build truly engaged communities on social media? We buy into pervasive and destructive myths and misconceptions about what social media is and how it works. Here are six of the most frequent social media myths that I come across in my work with nonprofits.

"Social media is free and easy."

Let's face it – back when social media first became popular, we were sold a bill of goods. Social media was once promised as the marketing silver bullet for nonprofits and brands. When Facebook rolled out the Business Page in November 2007, the social network touted it as the perfect way to stay in touch with fans and supporters. Some marketing experts even thought it would replace email marketing for good. Think of it: Setting up a Facebook Business Page completely free! It's so easy to use! Everyone is doing it! Start posting and like magic, the shares, the clicks, and the donations will just roll in!

When other social media channels started to become widely adopted for marketing purposes, the common belief was that we should all be using them, because they were "free" and "easy" and "everyone is on them." Board members and nonprofit directors started pressuring staff to take on "this social media stuff" – because it's free (and we know how much nonprofits LOVE free)! As we soon found out, social media is free like getting a puppy from your next door neighbor is free. In reality, marketing on social media it requires time, patience, willpower, creativity, and consistency to do it right; the principles are simple but getting results is certainly not "free and easy."

Nonprofit decision-makers and Board members have been guilty of buying into this myth, and of simply tacking social media tasks on to the already full plates of nonprofit staff. I once led a Board meeting where a trustee thought the solution to their funding shortfall was to create an Instagram account, because "it doesn't cost anything to set up and all the young donors are on there." I had to explain that just because these platforms are free to use and open to all, it does not automatically make them a fundraising solution. Just because you build it does not mean they will come.

"Social media is just about posting what you had for lunch."

I have been running my business successfully for 10 years, and I still get pushback from family and colleagues who think of social media marketing as a fake, made-up profession. Even the most renowned social media experts can suffer from the lack of outside respect for, or understanding of, their work.

These misconceptions are represented in a very accurate series of memes depicting life as a Social Media Manager. In such memes, there are six competing perspectives about social media management.

A What my friends think I do (drink the social media Kool-Aid).

B What my mom thinks I do (asleep at a desk).

C What society thinks I do (in bed on phone).

D What my executives think I do (lots of Facebook likes).

E What I think I do (a picture of a ninja).

F What I actually do (person sitting at a desk in front of a computer and coffee).

Getting appreciation and acknowledgement for your social media work can be challenging, especially in a sector that views marketing as "overhead" and not central to "the real work" – program work. In my experience, people outside the social media marketing field have an almost impossible time grasping the actual work that goes into building and managing online communities. They may use social media in their personal lives, but using it for marketing and fundraising requires different skillsets.

In addition to getting buy-in from your boss and your Board, it can also be just as hard to convince your co-workers that posting, tweeting, and storytelling has an effect on the bottom line. Acquiring a steady stream of photos, videos, and stories from program staff or from staff members and volunteers in the field can feel like pulling teeth, but is a required task to feed the insatiable social media beast.

"Social media requires skills in technology."

On the flip side of the "social media is easy and just for fun" mindset are those who believe that social media management requires a degree in computer science or a lot of tech-savvy know-how. This is not true! A person or organization can have all the degrees, tech skills, and fancy computer equipment in the world, but that does not mean that they will have a clue as to how to succeed in getting a group of people engaged on social media. Few individuals (technology pros included) innately understand how to use social media to build an online community. The best social media managers have a passion about the mission that is contagious, a knack for storytelling, and the ability to take risks and experiment. No internet technology or computer science degree required.

Audiences on social media crave authenticity, transparency, passion, and creativity, not a serious knowledge of the intricacies of the backend of each platform. All the things that nonprofits should be doing to build relationships with stakeholders, retain donors, and get more support, such as identifying and knowing their audience, being transparent, showcasing their success stories, asking for partners—that's what works on social media.

Take the example of The Ellie Fund, a small, bootstrapping nonprofit with a handful of paid staff and a hands-on Board of Directors in Boston, MA. In 2005, Julie Nations became The Ellie Fund's first full-time staff member. She managed all of their social media, communications, fundraising, and outreach. While Julie was not able to create flashy Facebook videos or build a fancy blog template, she had many strengths that translated perfectly into social media work: Telling her story of her mother's struggle

12

with breast cancer, communicating in a genuine, friendly way with supporters, conveying enthusiasm for her topic, and getting people excited about the work. Those are the reasons why The Ellie Fund kicks serious butt in the social media space.

The Centre Street Food Pantry in Newton, MA has one part-time paid staff member, and one social media account. They post daily on Instagram because the executive director loves to document visually the people who come into the food pantry and the great work done behind-the-scenes by the volunteers. Instagram was the easiest for them to immediately get set up and start using without taking a course, watching lengthy how-to videos, and acquiring technical skills.

This is an important point. All the tech know-how and computer skills in the world are not going to help your cause if you can't be authentic and interesting, and if you can't tell your story in a way that connects emotionally and inspires curiosity and compassion.

"Let's just get a young unpaid intern to manage it for us."

While some of us think that social media is worthless for marketing, and some think that it requires special technical skill, there is yet another group that firmly believes that any young person should be able to do it for us (for free).

Recently, I came across a job description in a nonprofit Facebook Group that looked like this:

Volunteer Social Media Intern, Unpaid, 25 hours per week
Required skills:
- Strong knowledge and understanding of the digital media landscape, including various social media websites.

- Strong critical thinking skills.
- Website redesign.
- Monitoring and management of organization blogs, forums, and social networks.
- Online outreach and promotion using Facebook, LinkedIn, Twitter, and more.
- Website and social media optimization.
- Keyword analysis.
- Cost/benefit analysis.
- Fearless attitude towards technology and a willingness to learn.

A 25-hour per week position, requiring all of these skills—for zero compensation? Honestly? Nonprofits, we can do better. Just because someone is young and just starting out does not mean that they should be taken advantage of. And just because they are young does not mean they were born with the skills required to carry out social media marketing campaigns, and to mobilize communities.

There are two pervasive and destructive attitudes that have infected many nonprofits, large and small, old and new. I call them the Cult of Free and the Cult of Young. The Cult of Free is when nonprofits feel entitled to receive all the things—labor, assets, items, knowledge—without putting any skin in the game. The Cult of Young is when they expect any young person they meet to gratefully accept these job offers for nothing, as they are assuredly an expert in all things social media, mobile, and technology.

So they call the Board member's 16-year-old niece or the director finds an unpaid college intern, and they expect them to set up and manage social media, and magically get instantaneous results. All without paying the person, figuring out what it really takes to succeed, or investing in the work.

The Cult of Free and the Cult of the Young are both insidious. Some organizations spend so much time and effort looking for free stuff and training young, inexperienced interns that they lose entire weeks of serving the community! This idea is completely bananas.

Yes, resources are stretched. Time and money are most often cited as the reasons why nonprofits do not improve their websites, tell their stories on Facebook, or use email software to communicate with supporters. In the digital age, nonprofits have to make some serious and difficult decisions about where to allocate resources and staff time. You can say that you value communicating with donors, sharing your impact with your community, and raising awareness with new groups of potential participants. But does your budget and your staff truly reflect this?

"Social media will get us more visibility."

You may think that the goal of social media, and the reason that you bought this book, is to "get more visibility" for your organization. It's not. Simply getting more people to be aware of you is not going to help you accomplish your bigger organizational goals. Getting more people to hear your voice does not necessarily mean that more people will listen.

If you had extra money in your marketing budget, would you purchase billboard space? Many nonprofits do, and it drives me crazy. I never understood the point of billboards to promote nonprofits and social causes. Billboards make sense to promote local restaurants, gas stations, that great store at the next exit, even radio stations (you can listen while driving). But for a cause? A social issue? Do billboards really work to drive donations or get people to go to your website? How can you measure the marketing ROI (return on investment) from a sign that is basically just yelling at strangers to pay attention?

This is how many nonprofits approach their social media platforms—as billboards to shout out one-way promotional messages, not as avenues to build relationships and make connections. They repeat: We are here! We got an award! We are awesome! Pay attention to us! But they don't offer any value in exchange for the attention they want to be paid. Fundraising guru Jeff Brooks was spot on when he wrote, "Proclaiming your existence is not fundraising. It's also not marketing, advertising, or branding."

"Social media, marketing, fundraising— isn't it all the same thing?"

Does this sound uncomfortably familiar to you? There is a common nonprofit practice of taking a successful, seasoned nonprofit fundraiser and out of the blue slap the 'social media manager' label to their job description. I've seen this treacherous "everything-but-programs" job description expanded in recent years, but the pay and the hours to do the job seem to remain fixed.

Social media marketing and fundraising should be in sync and not working at cross-purposes. In small shops these responsibilities may need to be coordinated and managed by just one person—I've been there, and there is no shame in this. However, the reality remains—marketing and fundraising require different strategies and unique skill sets, especially when it comes to leveraging social media.

On social media, nonprofit marketers should be risk-takers and attention-grabbers: gutsy, spirited, outspoken, with their fingers on the pulse of trends and movements. They should fully understand the target market they aim to reach, inside and out, and where to reach them, whether it be Facebook, Tumblr, or another platform. Nonprofit marketers are always asking: How can I get this message out to the widest number of people in my niche? How can I refine this message to not only grab attention but pique interest?

Nonprofit fundraisers are relationship builders. This does NOT mean they get to be boring and sit quietly in a corner, however! Effective nonprofit fundraisers are focused on opening up and maintaining the lines of communication with donors, creating partnerships around raising money and fiscal sustainability. These donors have already paid attention to the organization—enough so that they opened up their wallets and gave money, or they are being fostered to do so.

I have been a director of development/marketing/outreach (classic "everything but programs") in a small shop nonprofit, and I've had to build up all of these vital skillsets, often at the same time. The problem arises when nonprofit directors and supervisors casually tack-on social media responsibilities to already overflowing plates, assuming that the nonprofit professional in question was just born with these skills and knowledge (not to mention the time to carry them out).

Three Reality Checks for Nonprofit Marketers in the Digital Age

In the previous section we called out and shed light on the most destructive myths and misconceptions surrounding social media marketing in the nonprofit sector. But there are also harsh truths we must confront and address. Here are three reality checks that every social media manager, nonprofit and otherwise, will encounter in their work (and why we have to acknowledge and come to terms with them).

Humans are in information overload.

Our audience now suffers from a unique affliction of the digital age called "content shock," coined by Mark Schaefer in 2014. Content shock means that the sheer amount of information being thrown at our brains each day forces us to be more selective about where we dedicate our attention.

In his fantastic book *The Attention Merchants: The Epic Scramble to Get Inside Our Heads*, Tim Wu writes: "Every instant of every day we are bombarded by information... All told, every second, our senses transmit an estimated 11 million bits of information to our poor brains, as if a giant fiber-optic cable were plugged directly into them, firing information at full bore."

One study conducted at the University of California-San Diego, found that on the average day, humans are inundated with the equivalent amount of 34 gigabytes of data and information—enough to overload your standard laptop within a week.

Trying to compete and gain traction within that "giant fiber-optic cable" of information is our job as nonprofit communicators, advocates, and fundraisers. But most people are tuning out many messages as a matter of survival.

Digital distractions breed decision fatigue.

People make thousands of decisions about where they spend their time in a single day. We have to decide what to wear, what to eat, what to say, what to work on—the list is endless. In the digital age, this list increases exponentially. The average U.S. adult now uses an average of two mobile devices, plus a desktop computer. And these devices aren't idly sitting by, just waiting for us to pick them up—they are designed to steal our attention and our eyeballs! For most of us, our smartphone is an arm's reach away, constantly on, constantly pinging, begging you to pick it up.

Did you ever wonder why you are so bone-tired by the end of the day, even if you just sit at a computer? Partly, it is due to decision-fatigue. As nonprofit marketers, we are constantly switching gears, going to meetings, setting up campaigns, doing research, talking to coworkers, and much, much more. Brains burn more calories than any other organ—the brain makes up just 2% of the average human's body weight but consumes 20% of the energy we use in a single day. This is why the more we create, manage, and choose, the more tired we feel and the less able we are to discern between good choices and lazy ones.

Your supporters are busy, and in the digital age, they are pulled in an ever-expanding, relentless stream of notifications, asks, requests, and demands on their brain power and their time. Every day they are making many small decisions that all add up to brain exhaustion. Choosing to open up and read your email newsletter, deciding to share that Facebook post with a friend, making a determination on the amount to give to your online fundraising campaign—these seemingly small acts constitute workouts for the brain.

We cannot control the age of algorithms.

In the digital age, algorithms rule. Search engine algorithms comb the billions of pages of information on the web and decide in milliseconds which websites rank on the first page of Google. On social media, algorithms dictate which posts show up on a user's feed in which order, and which videos to play, based on viewing history and likelihood to watch the next video, and so on.

Facebook, Instagram, Twitter, LinkedIn, YouTube and the rest are constantly tweaking their algorithms to entice their users to spend more time on their sites by seeing more of the kinds of posts that will keep them there. This is why a smaller number of your fans and followers are seeing your posts. Not only is there simply too much information for them to be served all of it, the companies running the social media platforms want to focus on the most addictive types of content. Nonprofit marketers need to understand some basic concepts about how algorithms work and why social media posts and tweets are no longer chronological (and haven't been for a long time).

As a general rule, social media algorithms prioritize posts and tweets that receive a lot of discussion, engagement, and attention. Controversial and provocative topics, large international events, and clickbait news headlines always float to the top due to the amount of engagement they receive (positive and negative). The struggle for nonprofits in this environment is to stand out by creating and sharing content that is timely, relevant, and worthy of discussion so that it reaches more of the intended audience.

This may all seem like a very bleak landscape on which to build and mobilize a community. The good news is that *WE GOT THIS*. The digital tools may continually change, but nonprofits have been building communities and energizing constituencies through grassroots movements and word-of-mouth campaigns much longer than the social web has existed.

While the actual online tools may be frustrating, even infuriating, to nonprofits, the act of storytelling, genuinely communicating with supporters, and building an energized constituency shouldn't be. That's why I created this book. It should serve as your action guide—the How To, after understanding the bigger picture. In order to move forward, make effective changes, and do this work well, nonprofits have to tackle five essential marketing mindset shifts.

Five Essential
Marketing Mindset Shifts

As change agents, we have a responsibility to use revolutionary digital tools to change the world for the better. In our hyper-connected age, we have the ability like never before to influence global conversations around social justice, inequality, poverty, climate change, and other hot button issues. When used strategically, the connection and reach afforded by social media and the potential to persuade as well as mobilize is unparalleled.

To fully embrace the power of social media to change hearts and minds, to build movements, and to help more people, we need a tectonic shift in the nonprofit marketing mindset and practice. To create effective social media work we need an overhaul in how nonprofits communicate with stakeholders. Success demands that we articulate clearly what we stand for, define who we want to engage, and stop being afraid to run campaigns in an attention-grabbing way.

Using social media, nonprofits have the ability to:

- Shed light on complex, difficult issues.
- Advocate for our work and our impact.
- Address myths and misconceptions around the populations we serve.
- Educate and enlighten.
- Fill knowledge gaps.
- Keep people inspired by, and active in our work.
- Change the world we live in for the better.

My favorite definition of social media is as "computer-mediated technologies that facilitate the creation and sharing of information, ideas, career interests and other forms of expression via virtual communities and networks." Notice that it is NOT defined as "free and cheap ways to spread our promotional messages and get more people to our website." The point of creating "virtual communities and networks" to encourage "the creation and sharing of information and ideas" is vital.

Nonprofit marketers need to make the following five mindset shifts, and we have to work to correct these within the sector, if we are going to take back digital and create social change.

Stop blaming the technology.

We need to acknowledge the myths that we buy into and the snake oil that we were sold initially—and then we have to get over it. Let's overcome these hurdles, stop blaming the tools and the tech, and move forward into a better future.

If your marketing isn't working the way that you want it to, I'm willing to bet that your emails and social media posts are interrupting people who don't know you or trust you. We spend way too much time on choosing platforms and sending out promotions, and not nearly enough time sharing value and building community.

To quote Ice T: "Don't hate the player—hate the game." And what's the "game" in social media marketing? Grabbing attention and piquing interest. Getting seen and heard, and then getting people to listen and act. As we discussed earlier in this chapter, the internet can be a crowded, noisy, unforgiving place. Organic reach, meaning reach that you don't pay for with social ads, is experiencing a dramatic decline. Even old standards like email open and click-through rates are taking a nosedive.

However, this does not mean you get to just throw up your hands and say "Damn you, Zuckerberg!" and quit. The tools are just a symptom of the bigger problem. Many, many nonprofits and businesses and causes and individuals are using social media, email, blogging, and more to tell their stories, connect with customers and donors, and do business and raise money. For real-world nonprofit examples, check out the Shorty Social Good Awards, which honor the best of social media in the social sector, and PRNews' Nonprofit Awards, highlighting campaigns and communicators that get social media and multichannel campaigns right.

Stop saying that it's Facebook's fault, or Twitter's, or the email providers, or your website. Explore different tools if you need to. Get more training. Understand how best to leverage the digital tools at your disposal and then kick butt at using them. If you set up a telephone line in your office, but you never use it to reach out to donors, you can't blame the phone company when the money doesn't roll in.

Social media is a value exchange, pure and simple. Your audience gives you their time and attention and you have to give them something of value in return. You can't force people to join your movement—you can only entice their curiosity and then invite them in *on their terms*. Purchasing fans and followers, trading email lists, manipulating your audience with scare tactics, and engaging in smarmy, spammy digital behavior may get you a few more clicks in the short run. But in the long run, trust will evaporate as people begin to see through your cheap tricks.

There are no shortcuts here. Effective social media marketing requires understanding your audience and how you can add unique value to their busy lives. Content such as helpful blogs, educational videos, and thoughtful social media posts can help you spread your ideas to people that will be receptive, enthusiastic, and excited to join you. Recognizing this value exchange is the only way to build an audience online with integrity.

Social media marketing that works is not about interrupting people with flashy website pop-ups or clickbait headlines. It's consciously creating something that your audience wants, in return for something you want—their attention, their trust, and eventually, their action. If you are simply using these channels to push out promotional messages and advertisements, your supporters will never feel proud to be a part of your work.

The digital revolution is here, and it's not going away. The only way to "cut through the clutter" in the digital age is to make yourself indispensable and valuable to a smaller, more targeted group of people. The kind of people that would miss you if you went away.

End imposter syndrome.

Some of the most famous social media movements were started with an individual and a smartphone. From Tahrir Square, to

#MeToo, to #BlackLivesMatter, the Ice Bucket Challenge, and #MarchForOurLives, viral campaigns and entire world-changing movements have been built using these people-powered platforms.

Now, any individual or group of activists with a great new idea, a passionate outlook, and some access to technology and the internet can reach millions. Institutions and organizations aren't always in the forefront of these digital movements, but we can learn from them. Today, successful nonprofits and social causes are embracing and learning from these campaigns and the ways in which they leverage technology to connect like-minded people for the purpose of change. In her brilliant book *Twitter and Tear Gas: The Power and Fragility of Networked Protest*, Zeynep Tufekci writes, "There is no doubt that social media platforms are fully reshaping how movements connect, organize, and evolve during their lifespan."

So you don't have cute puppies and children to feature in your social media content. So what? You need to get creative! Your supporters care about your cause and the work that you do. Stop comparing yourself to the organizations with huge marketing departments and an endless list of celebrity supporters. There is a reason that your unique cause exists and there are a myriad of reasons that people support your work. Focus on building upon what you have, not lamenting what you don't have.

Think like a journalist.

I feel incredibly fortunate to have earned my Bachelor of Science in magazine journalism before the proliferation of social media and smartphones. Being able to experience college without the societal pressure of looking perfect on Instagram was undoubtedly a personal blessing, but also a professional one. I love that I was able to truly learn the core principles of journalism in a time when everyone wasn't glued to their mobile apps. (Insert the "kids today!" grumpy old person joke.)

The late David Brudnoy, iconic radio talk show host and outspoken AIDS activist, taught my favorite journalism class at Boston University. Professor Brudnoy never accepted excuses for boring, poorly-researched and badly-written stories. His opinion was that anyone who is trying to communicate should think like a journalist, trying to find the hook that will not only make people pay attention, but also make them curious.

In today's hyper-connected, always-on digital age, nonprofit marketers need to think of themselves as journalists and documentarians. We all need to be looking for the interesting angle and the emotional hook that will captivate our audience and get them wanting to learn more.

What are the skills required of a great journalist? They are much the same as we would expect in a stellar nonprofit social media manager:

- Forward-thinking skills—Always pondering what is new and fresh, what is on the horizon, what is provocative.
- Interview skills—The ability to draw interesting, unexpected information and great storytelling out of people.
- Investigative skills—Being willing and able to sniff out stories and dig for information relevant to the audience and to the community.
- Writing skills—Skill in crafting and composing tweets, posts, captions to photos, and the like is vital to communicate the message and get the point across.

- Nuance—Understanding context and nuance and the ability to remain agile and respond quickly to changes in the landscape.
- Team players—Nonprofit social media managers should be sharing their education and professional knowledge, building up other staff members and volunteers instead of operating in a silo, or excluding others.

Visuals are imperative on social media channels. They are more important than text in most cases. Digital marketing success requires grit, authenticity, and the willingness to take risks. There is a science to it, but a lot of it is experimentation, humor, and "edu-tainment" (education/entertainment). Grabbing attention means being provocative, interesting, and relevant. It means getting out of your comfort zone and trying new things, like Facebook Live or Instagram Stories. Social media success requires persistence and constantly looking out for great photos, compelling video stories, and mission moments to keep your audience wanting more.

Be transparent.

If you want to keep your nonprofit operations and impact in the shadows, you are not ready to jump on social networks. Nonprofit organizations that do not want to publicize their programs, their success stories, and their services should not get on social media. Social media is all about transparency—it is a perfect place for your supporters to learn more about your leadership, your back office, your staff, and your organization's values and processes.

Social media means that you are opening up a two-way dialogue with constituents, donors, volunteers and the general public. Once you open up this delicious can of worms, you can't "un-open" it. People on social media channels expect answers and acknowledgement, and fast.

You may not be ready for social media if you don't want to open up conversations and build authentic relationships with your community online.

Do the work.

You may think your nonprofit has most of this "social media stuff" all figured out, and what you really need is just a bulleted list of tips to quickly get more Facebook fans. In my experience leading digital marketing teams at nonprofits, and building out assessments and training programs that get results, your simply acquiring more fans, clicks, or likes is not enough to build an online movement that stands the test of time.

You may also think that social media can be completely automated. Sure, I'm all for scheduling tweets here and there, and strategically using certain platforms to streamline the work-flow. Automation tools have their uses and can save time and increase results when used strategically and thoughtfully. However, nonprofits that effectively use social media need to budget some of their work day to monitor conversations on their social channels and respond in real time. If you are not willing to use each channel the way it is meant to be used (and they are all vastly different), and you simply want to send the same announcement to each channel and never check it again, do us all a favor and don't use social media.

Our Moral Obligation to #TakeBackDigital

In just the last few years, the world has seen social media go from being lauded as protecting democracy and upending dictatorships in the Middle East to being blamed for swaying the election in the U.S., or to an increase in cyberbullying, suicide rates, and anxiety and depression. Every day brings flashy headlines regarding data breaches, privacy concerns, censorship, and other important issues that are front and center in a world where sharing ideas and being connected is easier than ever.

Seth Godin writes that we live in "a moment in time when more people are connected and few are trusted." Trust in civic institutions, government, and nonprofits is at its lowest point in history. Edelman Digital released a report showing the following discouraging statistics about public trust:

- Just one-third of Americans trust their government "to do what is right";

- 42% of Americans trust the media (down from 47% a year ago); and
- Trust in nonprofits/NGOs is higher than trust in government, but it still decreased by nine percentage points from last year.

Most shockingly, the firm has been doing this same report every year for 18 years, and has never before recorded such a steep decrease in trust.

I would also argue that facts and truth are endangered. We live in an age where science, data, and research are persistently challenged and absurdly politicized by partisan hacks and self-proclaimed "experts". Feeling true connection online is also rare. People who do manage to create authentic connections over social media report having a largely positive experience. Users who are on social media as a genuine way to stay in touch with people they care about do not report the same levels of anxiety or depression as others. The problem is when we confuse likes or reach with true connection—they are NOT the same thing.

In light of this, it is my belief that nonprofits have a moral obligation to engage authentically on social media, both to increase trust in institutions and to connect people with the causes and issues they care most about. *We need the voice of the third sector to advocate for those who don't have a voice.* We need the strength of our convictions to educate, inform, and build support on behalf of problems that cannot and will not be addressed by the market or by the government. We need to make the digital world a better, more ethical space to discover, to learn, and to connect.

Nonprofits have a distinct and unique responsibility to their stakeholders and constituents to educate, to inspire, and to build community. We need to address fake news about our cause head-on, to provide reliable and trusted resources, and to advocate for our missions. We must communicate what we stand for and stand firm on our core values—even if it means getting a handful of people upset. We should make it as easy as possible for the largest group possible to participate in our work, and that means meeting stakeholders where they are. And where they are *is* on social media.

Are You One of Us?

This book is for those of us sick of the nonprofit social media status quo. We are tired of spinning our wheels, chasing shiny new objects, and posting to the sound of crickets. We know that we are changing lives and making an impact, that we have a community of people who love us and could help us spread the word about our work, and that we have compelling messages to spread if we could only figure out the best and most effective way to share them.

When used thoughtfully and strategically, entire movements can be built using digital tools, with just passion, a great idea, and a smartphone. Ideas can spread like wildfire, changing hearts and minds, opening up worldviews, inspiring debate and discussion. Some of the best reasons to start a nonprofit social media marketing campaign:

- You want to get out of your gated castle and increase transparency.
- You want people to see what you do, who you are, and why you do it.

- You want to solicit feedback on a product, program, or service.
- You want to see your organization through a new lens and get a fresh perspective.
- You want to be more alert and responsive to conversations about your cause.
- You want to inform and to catalyze current marketing and fundraising efforts.

Beyond pushing out marketing messages, what nonprofits share on social media affirms our values, our belief systems, and helps us reach more people who think like us and may want to get involved in our work. Showcasing impact and telling great stories about our mission and vision is a great way to deepen relationships with existing supporters and hopefully get them to bring others on board.

The stories and communications we share with our supporters explain what we stand for, what we are trying to change, and help to expose our core values to a wider variety of people. A lot of people will understand our world view and want to get on board. Many will not, and that's fine. I believe that even though we don't have huge marketing departments with large budgets, small nonprofits have a distinct advantage in the social media space: Rather than selling perfume or designer bags, *we are selling a better world.*

How This Book Works

O ur first step together is an agreement. You agree to go on this journey, to roll up your sleeves and get your hands dirty, to think critically, and to embrace creativity and new ideas. I agree to provide you with a framework to revamp, revitalize, and recharge your social media efforts in just 90 days.

The good news is that dramatically improving your results on social media isn't rocket science. The principles and the path to success are simple to grasp and to embrace. However, actually implementing the work and putting the plan into practice isn't easy. There are no silver bullets. There is no get-rich-quick scheme. Success on social media requires thought, purpose, planning, and a bit of elbow grease and innovation. I know that you can do it!

This book is divided up into three 30-day sections. After each section, you will complete a section of your Nonprofit Social Media Blueprint. The Blueprint will provide you with the infrastructure and required action steps necessary to level up your social media game and start activating your audience.

SECTION 1: CLARIFY

During days 1-30 we will:

A. Determine your primary goal, identify the audience you need to reach to accomplish the goal, and brainstorm the unifying message for your social media work;

B. Select the best social media strategies and platforms to use, based on your organizational capacity and resources;

C. Identify and prioritize tasks, to prevent overwhelm and to gain focus; and

D. Learn ways to build a nonprofit culture that understands and embraces social media work, including creating internal and external policies.

SECTION 2: CAPTIVATE

During days 31-60 we will:

1. Choose the most effective types of content that your nonprofit needs to create and share on social media, based on the Six Pillars;

2. Review 10 ways to effectively repurpose your existing content, as well as a simple methodology to curate relevant outside content for your audience; and

3. Address some of the most common social media challenges that get nonprofits stuck, and offer solutions to keep you moving forward.

SECTION 3: CULTIVATE

During days 61-90, we will:

A. Determine your social media cadence—how much and how often you will post;

B. Fill out your Social Media Calendar for the next 30 days; and

C. Explore advanced ways to amplify your social media messaging and reach more people.

To wrap-up, I'll give you tips on keeping engagement and enthusiasm up between specific marketing campaigns, and ways to measure your progress to ensure forward momentum and growth. At the end of our 90 days together, you will have the confidence and focus to go forward and slay social media!

Now let's get to work!

Part One

CLARIFY

"What's your flag? Why would someone fly it?"
—Seth Godin

What you need to complete this section:
- A copy of the Nonprofit Social Media Blueprint—download it at www.jcsocialmarketing.com/socialmediabook

Introduction

The theme for the first 30 days of our work together is "Clarify." In order to make sure your social media house is built on a solid foundation, we have to create a concrete and actionable Nonprofit Social Media Blueprint to follow as a guide. Readers of this book can get their very own printable copy of the Blueprint at www. jcsocialmarketing.com/socialmediabook.

Why use the Nonprofit Social Media Blueprint? Blueprints are detailed plans and specifications used by builders and contractors as instruction manuals. A blueprint describes the required materials needed to complete a building to the agreed-upon specifications, which can then be used to estimate *the time* that it will take and *the total cost* involved. Good stuff to know before starting out! Your Nonprofit Social Media Blueprint will serve as your instruction manual and guidebook to revamping your social media or to building it from the ground up, showing you how to construct and connect the various elements that go into a social media strategy.

To set your nonprofit up for maximum effectiveness on social media, you need to be crystal clear on your definition of social media success. Your definition is different from the nonprofit down the street, is different from a local business, and is different from a major brand with a huge budget. Goal-setting includes a close examination of where you want to go, who you need to bring along, and what you need them to do in order to achieve success and build the type of social media house you want. In Chapter 1, you will set clear goals for your social media work. This is the first and most vital step of the process, because if you do not know what you want to build, how can you create a blueprint to construct it?

Chapter 2 will tackle what is often the hardest part of social media planning for nonprofits—identifying a target audience. I know, I know (trust me)—your nonprofit has 10+ different audiences that you need to communicate with on a regular basis. This is normal. But, in order to get traction on social media, identifying a focal point—a target audience—is critical for you to define *where* you spend your time on social media, *how often* you will post, and *what* you will post about. If you don't know who you are talking to, how will you know what to say and how to say it?

Message clarification and refinement is the focus of Chapter 3. What do you want people to do? What action do you want them to take? What are you going to say that will inspire and mobilize your target audience—so much so, that they take the action that you want? How can you say it in a way that will get them from passive to passionate?

It is only after you have successfully defined these three areas—goals, target audience, and message—that you can brainstorm the unique strategies, platforms, and digital tools to employ. Most people are impatient and want to get right to the tweeting, the Instagramming, the livestreaming—and I appreciate that enthusiasm. However, creating a plan with a jump-right-in, "tools first, strategy last" mentality is probably what got you into this mess in the first place. Until you know exactly what you want to accomplish, whom you need to spur into action, and what you need to say to get them engaged, you will just be spinning your wheels on social media for little to no results.

Chapters 4 and 5 walk you through how to choose the best social media strategies to use to accomplish your goal—and more importantly, how to jettison the rest. No FOMO (fear of missing out) here! You will evaluate and select the best social media platforms, based on a quick primer of the top five most popular platforms for nonprofits, and a quick assessment of your own capacity, budget, and resources. While nonprofits often want to jump headlong into the platforms and tools as a first step, this work comes at the tail end of planning. How can you know which tools to use if you don't know what kind of house you are going to build, and where?

CHAPTER 1

Setting Clear Goals

Goal-setting is my favorite part of the work, but this isn't true for many of my nonprofit clients. It can be difficult and time-consuming to evaluate where you are now as opposed to where you want to go. I start with goals because they are the North Star of your entire social media plan. Your goals are the WHY—the purpose and the reason that drive your digital efforts. If your journey on social media is successful, your goal is your destination. To maximize your limited time and resources (not to mention your creativity and brain power), it is a best practice to focus on one overarching goal for your first Nonprofit Social Media Blueprint. I understand that nonprofits often have multiple goals in their marketing work, so you may require separate (but complementary) Blueprints for each distinct goal.

A note about marketing vs. fundraising: While I often advocate that no nonprofit employee or volunteer should operate in a silo, I also staunchly believe that social media marketing and social media fundraising are very different goals and thus involve different target audiences, strategies, platforms, and tactics to work. Great marketing grabs attention, piques interest, and casts a wide net to bring in as many fish as possible. Effective fundraising ensures that those fish feel appreciated, and that they stay involved and inspired for the long run. (And that they are caught again and again! Ok, enough with the fish metaphor, ew.) But for *both* to work, nonprofits need compelling stories, crystal clear messaging, and a good sense of who their supporters are and who they want to attract to be a part of the work. (Read on for specific ways to do just that!)

Some common goals for nonprofits using social media:

1. Engaging our community to keep people inspired by and active in our work.
2. Recruiting and engaging participants to use our programs or services.
3. Supporting event fundraising (galas, walks, etc.).
4. Brand building and reputation management for the organization.
5. Supporting major donor fundraising and annual giving.
6. Raising awareness of our issues to educate people on our cause.
7. Supporting fundraising from individuals making small to medium gifts.

Each of these goals are distinct, and each require their own Nonprofit Social Media Blueprint to be fully realized and to attain the maximum of success. Certainly, there is some overlap, but the audience and the message for each are distinct, and thus the strategies and platforms will vary. But don't dismay—once you create one Blueprint and walk through all of the steps, it will become easier to create another.

A WORD OF CAUTION: Your goal should not simply be to "raise awareness" or "increase visibility." Awareness without action is not worth very much. As marketing expert Seth Godin said, "Everyone reading this is aware that turnips are a root vegetable. But knowing they exist doesn't mean you're going to have them for dinner."

Let's dig deeper into the goal of "raising awareness" since it is so commonly cited in nonprofit marketing plans. *Why* do you want awareness raised? *Why* is getting more visibility important? What will you do with this increased knowledge of your organization? What could you accomplish if more people simply knew more about your work?

We can improve upon the overused goal of "raised awareness". What about changing it to: We will leverage social media to share helpful resources, explain our unique impact, and connect our donors to our mission. In this way, we will become an indispensable part of the community, so much so that even people that do not directly use our services and benefit from our programs would miss us if we were gone.

Another example: *We will use social media to build an active and motivated online community that is energized and willing to support our work.*

One more: *We will inspire our supporters to share our work with their networks, thus gathering new people into the fold that will support our work.*

I should say that there is demonstrable evidence that the mere act of elevating an issue and getting it into the public eye can create an environment where real change is possible. (It's rare, but it does happen.) If a critical mass of people are shown real-world examples of the reality on the ground as well as the vision for the future, they are more likely to have empathy and understanding of the issue and the people involved. This is certainly true of LGBTQ+ marriage equality movement, the #TransRights movement, the #MeToo and #TimesUp phenomenons, and more. But for many small nonprofits focused on specific local or regional issues, a lot of critical money, time and effort is wasted on simply "making a splash" or "raising awareness," while the societal problems they are trying to solve persist.

Nonprofit Social Media Blueprint: Clearly articulate what you hope to accomplish by using social media for your nonprofit.

CHAPTER 2

Audience Identification

Who are you talking to on social media? It may surprise you to know that the correct answer is not "everyone with a pulse and a bank account." Before choosing digital platforms, mobile apps, and video editing software, you need to understand and be able to identify the needs and behaviors of your target audience. By "target audience," I mean the group of people with whom your nonprofit aims to engage on social media, towards the ultimate accomplishment of your goal.

To demonstrate just some of the benefits of target audience identification on social media, I'll share a client story about Road Scholar, formerly Elderhostel, a nonprofit in Boston, MA. Their mission is to inspire adults to learn, discover, and travel. When they came to us they had been posting inconsistently on social media for about a year, slowly growing their fan base but not at the rate that they wanted. They also were getting very little engagement from their posts, and they wanted to understand why.

The problem was that they didn't understand who they were talking to on social media, why these people would pay attention to them, nor did they have identified goals for their efforts. We helped them set social media goals and then identify the target audience that they would need to reach to accomplish their goals. You cannot effectively figure out who you want to reach if you don't know why you are communicating with them.

In the beginning, Road Scholar's goal was simply "to raise awareness of and interest in their educational learning trips for older adults." To better help them get more engagement and shares, especially on Facebook, we needed to create an audience persona— a made-up amalgamation of a person that encapsulated all the characteristics of their ideal social media community member. After analyzing their donor base, the people who took their educational trips, and their social media audience, we created this persona. We called her "the Funky Grandma."

The Funky Grandma is an older woman who likes to learn, likes to travel, and enjoys adventure. She is interested in women's issues and advocating for older adults. Creating and sharing engaging content became much easier and more intuitive once Road Scholar knew who they were speaking to on social media. Every post has to pass one test: Would the Funky Grandma like it? If so, it's posted. If not, it's reworked. Road Scholar's engagement on Facebook skyrocketed, with a 500% increase in engagement and a doubling of their fans and followers within a year of using this persona to create and vet social media posts.

It's important to note that just because all social media posts are designed with the Funky Grandma in mind, *they do not exclusively appeal to just one segment of Road Scholars' diverse supporter network.*

Targeted messaging does not necessarily exclude other groups that may also be interested in the content. For example, I often enjoy Road Scholars' Facebook posts, and I am about 25 years younger than the target demographic. Having a specific, well-defined person in mind when you share on social media will dramatically help your focus and prevent you from throwing stuff up to see what sticks, but it won't stop others from liking it also.

So how can your nonprofit identify your own target audience persona, similar to the Funky Grandma? Target audience identification involves three main parts:

1. First, refer back to the goal that you set for your nonprofit on social media. Which group is best suited to help you accomplish your goal?

2. Second, do some research to figure out who is already with you on social media. Which segments already make up your social media communities?

3. Third, think about who you aspire to connect with on social media. *This group must be aligned with your goals and cannot simply be an audience you hope to engage because your Board told you to, or because you read a newspaper article about Millennials.* Ask: Why is this audience vital to achieving your goals? Where does this particular group of people spend time online?

Refer Back to Your Goal

Look back at the goal you wrote down on your Nonprofit Social Media Blueprint. Think strategically about the group of people that you need to reach in order to accomplish this particular goal. Different goals require reaching out to and engaging different audiences. Different audiences respond to different messages and participate on different social media platforms. Complete strangers who know nothing about your work are much less likely to donate and to volunteer their time than a group of people who follow you on social media, have made a donation already, and signed up to get your email updates or attend your events.

Use the table below as a guideline and example to follow when matching your target audience segment to your social media goal.

Goal	Target Audience
(Example) To use social media to become an indispensable part of the community, so much so that even people that do not directly use our services and benefit from our programs would miss us if we were gone.	(Example) People who know us and love us and may be willing to spread the word to others. People who know a little bit about us and want to learn more. Community members involved in our work who have influence, including legislators, media contacts, partner organizations.
(Example) To build an active and motivated online community ready and willing to support our work and advocate for our issue.	(Example) Current online audience members who have advocated for us in the past or indicated an interest in advocacy.
(Example) To drive donations for our year-end fundraising campaign.	(Example) Current donors and prospects, lapsed donors, staff, Board, volunteers.

Nonprofit Social Media Blueprint: Identify the main group or groups of people that you will need to reach in order to accomplish the goal. Refer to the examples cited in the book.

Who Is Already With Us?

Unless you are starting 100% from scratch with no database, email list, and social media accounts, you already have a group of people (even if it's a small group) who have raised their hands to say that they want to hear more from you. When revamping your social media strategy, it's a heck of a lot easier to focus on the group of people who have already opted in than trying to grab the attention and interest of complete strangers.

To learn about the demographic makeup and other characteristics of your current digital and social media following, you can:

1. Use the insights and analytics already available within each social media platform.

If you have a presence on any major social media platforms, and if you have administrator privileges to the account, you have access to information about your audience, your content performance, and more. Looking at Twitter Analytics, Facebook and Instagram Insights, and the back-end of your emails can help provide a clearer picture of your current fans and followers.

Three buckets of information to look for in your analytics:

- What is the demographic makeup of your fans? Age, location, gender? Where do they predominantly reside, in which time zones?

- Which topics tend to elicit the most engagement? What spurs the greatest amount of comments and share? What gets a lot of likes or reactions?

- Which types of content—photo, video, text—generally get the most engagement? When you post a link to an article, does that resonate more than a text update? Do people love your video content? Does live video work better than recorded video?

2. Sign up for a basic social media measurement tool.

Free and low-cost social media management and measurement tools, such as HootSuite or Buffer, can help you run basic reports on your audience demographics and other characteristics. Most social media management and measurement tools allow for a free 30-day trial, and many have nonprofit discounts. You can also explore investing in a more robust (and more costly) social media measurement platform, such as HubSpot or Sprout Social, to acquire more detailed information to match to your database and your records.

3. Ask your audience directly.

Interact offline with your online community! Call them on the phone, send a postcard, ask at an in-person event, host a Facebook live. Conduct a poll on Facebook, Instagram, Twitter, LinkedIn, SurveyMonkey—anywhere you can reach out to your current audience.

You can also send out a simple email survey to get a better picture of your current stakeholders and their online habits. Sample questions may include:

    a. Are you familiar with social media? Social media includes but is not limited to Facebook, LinkedIn, Twitter, YouTube, blogs, etc.

    b. If yes, which social media sites do you interact with? List the top 10 to 12 social media sites and platforms.

c. How much time do you spend engaging in social media per week? How much is personal use? How much is professional use?

d. What would motivate you to interact with our brand in social media? (entertaining videos, helpful content, impact stories, etc.)

e. What other brands or organizations do you engage with on social media? This could take the form of blogs that you read, Facebook fan pages, or Twitter feeds that you follow.

If you need more information on your target audience, more comprehensive online surveys could be the answer. I also suggest reading the incredibly valuable book *Ask* by Ryan Levesque for in-depth methodology on surveying and segmenting your audience.

4. Speak their language.

Important note: Speak your target audience's language! Write down their answers to your questions and their comments using their words—not what you think they should be saying, or the words that you want them to use. This will help you in the next step as you craft a message specifically for them.

Real-world example: When I worked as the Development and Marketing Manager at a small community-based nonprofit in Virginia, I was tasked with creating a public awareness campaign around intimate partner violence. The goal was to get people to call our 24-hour emergency hotline and access the free resources on our website. We were promoting the use of the term "intimate partner violence" because we knew that not every survivor or victim lives with their abuser and this term is more inclusive and representative than the term "domestic violence". However, we discovered that hardly anyone in our target audience group was searching the internet or asking their health care providers for "intimate partner violence" resources or help. Instead, searches and enquiries using the traditional terms "domestic violence" and "spouse abuse" were 10x more popular that any other term on this issue. In order to best reach our target audience—people in abusive situations—and accomplish our goal of encouraging them to seek help, we changed the wording on our website, social media, and promotional materials back to "domestic violence".

Nonprofit Social Media Blueprint: List at least two methods that you are going to use to help you find out more about your existing social media audience. Examples: Twitter Analytics, Facebook Insights, donor surveys, phone calls, email polls, etc.

Who Else Do We Need to Reach?

To reach your goal, you may need to target a completely new audience on social media—people that have never heard of you. This may not be true for those of us who simply want to increase donor retention, or get people already on our email list to call their legislators, or drive people from our Facebook Page to our website. Your current community and supporters may be enough to get you to your goal.

Your Nonprofit Social Media Blueprint may have a goal that requires reaching a brand new audience, people who are not currently engaged with you, people that are not aware of your programs and services. Since you are not as familiar with this new audience and they are not acquainted with you, you need to do some dedicated research. Determine where the target audience is that you aspire to connect with and engage. This ties directly back to your goals for using social media, because you want to target an audience that is likely to take the action that you desire.

For example, if one of your goals is to build up your peer-to-peer fundraising program, but your current audience is made up of baby boomers and matures, you may need to target younger donors more comfortable with technology and social media fundraising. If you want to start a text advocacy campaign, and your supporters don't have smartphones, trying to reach civically-engaged digital natives, 20 and 30-year-olds comfortable with mobile technology, may be your desired audience.

If you have determined that you need to reach and engage an entirely new audience, answer the following questions:

- Why is this target audience important?
- How will they help you accomplish your goal?
- What action do you want them to take?
- Who is most likely to take this action?
- What might they already know about you?
- What may drive them to take the action that you want?
- Where do they get their information?
- What else is important to them in creating a meaningful life and how can your nonprofit fit in?
- Where do they spend their time online?

Conduct demographic research to ascertain where this group spends time online. For example, Pew Research Center releases frequent reports and analysis of adult social media usage in the United States. In their 2018 Social Media Use Report, they found:

- Roughly two-thirds of U.S. adults (68%) now report that they are Facebook users, and roughly three-quarters of those users access Facebook on a daily basis.

- YouTube is now used by nearly three-quarters of U.S. adults and 94% of 18- to 24-year-olds.
- 35% of U.S. adults now say they use Instagram.
- Around four-in-ten (42%) adults ages 65 and older now report owning smartphones.

Pew also publishes helpful demographic breakdowns and usage reports for all of the major digital platforms. Some ways to use this wealth of data:

- Is your nonprofit creating an engagement strategy for young professionals? Find out where they spend time. Instagram and Snapchat may be your best bet.
- Are you targeting people in their mid-40s to learn more about financial assistance? YouTube, Facebook, and LinkedIn reign supreme with this age group.
- Want to get more new mothers on board? Pinterest is popular with women, especially women with young children.

Nonprofit Social Media Blueprint: Determine where your target audience is. Be sure that you are able to tie this audience directly back to your goals for using social media, because you want to target people likely to take the desired action.

What Drives Them to Act?

One of my favorite marketing bloggers, Neil Patel, proposes that the job of all communicators involves just three steps:

- Understand what your audience needs and craves.
- Understand what drives them and what keeps them up at night.
- Use this information to influence their behavior.

Simple, right? This is what the big brands and technology companies are doing to your brain right now—drilling down into your motivations, your wants and desires, and then leveraging this knowledge to sell you relevant products and services.

Beyond understanding simple demographics, getting real engagement and participation from your social media community requires an understanding of the things that drive them to make decisions. Even if you are starting from scratch, it's important to determine the characteristics and desires of your target audience so that you can craft a message that will speak to them.

When you understand what motivates people, it's easier to get them to take the action you want. Behavioral science research has shown that there are three key motivating factors that the majority of people share:

1. The first is purpose. Most people want to do work and contribute to causes that are meaningful to them, and that are worthy of their time and attention. People often feel a need to connect their own specific individual context to the overall mission of the organizations they support and their places of employment.

2. The second is a desire for growth. People want to learn new things and feel challenged, or many will lose motivation.

3. The third motivating factor is connection. Don't you want to be connected with people that you admire, trust, and respect? Most people do too.

Some questions to ask when painting a picture of your target audience on social media:

- Does your audience primarily value purpose, growth, or connection?

- Do they feel that taking an action on your behalf is meaningful?
- Do they want to grow their knowledge on the issue? If so, how?
- Do they want to connect with other people who feel as passionate as they do about the cause?

Determine what motivates your community and you will be well on your way to crafting messages and selecting the appropriate strategies that will resonate. *Example: In order to accomplish our goal of building an active and motivated online community ready and willing to support our work and advocate for our issue, we need to reach people interested in the issue and in our solution. We want them to sign up for our email list to get more information and to develop a relationship with us. To drive this action, we can inspire them with great storytelling via email and by sharing evidence of our impact.*

Nonprofit Social Media Blueprint: Write down three motivating factors that will spur your supporters into action. Then complete the "fill in the blanks" activity to put it all together using the Nonprofit Social Media Blueprint at www.jcsocialmarketing.com/ socialmediabook.

CHAPTER 3

A Message that Attracts

"If you stand for nothing, Burr, then what will you fall for?"
—**Lin-Manuel Miranda** in *Hamilton*

Attention is the scarcest resource on the planet. There is no doubt that we are living in an attention economy—fighting for survival against internet algorithms, big brand budgets, lighting-fast news cycles, and more. However, even in this noisy and cluttered digital reality, we do seem to be able to focus our attention on what we deem important. Book sales are up year-over-year and physical book sales are thriving. We binge-watch for hours on Netflix and Amazon Prime shows, we still go to movies, concerts, plays—all places that demand our attention for hours at a time.

In the attention economy, no one owes you their attention, you have to earn it. Attention cannot be purchased the same way that it could five, 10, 20 years ago, when we had a handful of TV channels to entertain us. The traditional, old-fashioned ways of grabbing (a.k.a. stealing) attention do not work now. We simply have too many options. It's not the 1950s and you cannot Don Draper yourself to success by yelling at strangers via billboards, purchased email lists, random mailings, and the like.

Manipulating people and tricking them into spending their most precious resource—attention—does not lead to trust, and won't result in long-term marketing success. Deceiving people with flashy ads or click-bait headlines certainly won't build long-term sustainable relationships with members, supporters, and donors—the lifeblood of most nonprofits.

So how can a small nonprofit "cut through the clutter" online? The short answer? You can't. The longer answer? You shouldn't worry about it. Clutter in the digital age just means a variety of choices as to where we place our attention. Most of the stuff published online— articles, videos, posts, and the rest—are full of spam, provide very little insight and value, and should be ignored. Some pieces of communication are valuable, and should be shared widely—that's where you want your nonprofit to be.

So the question should NOT be how do we spend more money and more time and more resources to "cut through the clutter" and steal the attention of strangers who most likely won't participate in our cause. The question should be: *How do we cultivate, nurture, and inspire a wildly passionate group of supporters that actually care about what we do?*

The only way to stand out is to matter to the right group of people, so much so that they spread the word about you to their networks. And the only way to matter is to stay true to your core beliefs, and to stand up for what you believe in—encouraging your online community to come along for the ride.

A great example is the #ForEveryGirl campaign. In 2015, the Queen Anne Girl Scouts of Western Washington received a $100,000 donation from an anonymous donor. The only problem? The donor stipulated that "our gift will not be used to support transgender girls." Instead of keeping quiet, the Girl Scouts decided to take a stand for their core value that "Girls Scouts is for every girl." They returned the money and made a public appeal to recoup the $100K via crowd-funding—and their supporters responded, by raising over $250K. In staying steadfastly loyal to their brand's mission and values, the Girl Scouts were able to turn a negative situation into an opportunity to advocate for social justice, as well as involve their community. They made people feel proud to be Girl Scouts. And anyone who disagreed with this stance? Well, they were in the minority. And they never would have become loyal supporters in the long-run.

The only solution to the digital clutter problem is to craft inspiring, relevant communications designed for your target audience, asking them for their attention and earning their participation. This is why we spent so much time in the previous section identifying who you are engaging with and what action you want them to take—different messages inspire different actions.

It's important to understand that no matter how popular and well-known you are, social media marketing can be a frustrating endeavor. Not everyone, not even half of your fans and followers, will end up taking the action that you want. That's ok. If you have been consistently showing up for your supporters, demonstrating impact, creating connections, and providing valuable insight, then they are much more likely to act on your behalf when asked.

Don't worry about the masses. Focus your social media efforts on your community and on your goals. If your message is good enough, inspiring enough, and creative enough, some of your audience members will share it with their networks. It's important to embrace, acknowledge, and cultivate the people who have raised their hand and said, yes, we want to hear from you. We want to go on this journey with you. We are interested. Show us more.

Write Your Manifesto

As nonprofit marketers, getting people to our website, to sign up for our email list, to read our blog posts, to watch our Facebook videos is our primary job—that's what we do. But we can't do any of this if our message is boring, spammy, or even if it just elicits an "oh, that's nice. (delete)." The problem here is that in order to stand out, we have to take risks. We have to be timely, relevant, urgent, interesting, and provocative. There is no other way to do effective marketing in the digital age.

As I have said time and time again, the nonprofits who articulate and stand by their core values, even if their core values bother some people, are the ones who attract the most passionate group around them. Here are some more tips for a compelling nonprofit message:

- Don't be afraid to take a stand for what you believe in. Your cause means something.
- Show off your personality and your voice. What makes you human?
- Demonstrate what sets you apart and makes you different from the pack. Are there other nonprofits doing similar work or serving similar populations? Figure out what is unique about you and showcase that.
- Know who you *are* as definitively as who you *are not*.
- Know you want to attract as well as who you do not.

A great message attracts the right groups of people and draws them in, but it also repels the wrong people—the people who don't believe what you believe, and no matter what, they aren't going to take the action that you need. All of this is ok! If you try to appeal to everyone, you will appeal to no one. It makes much more sense to attract the best prospects with a message designed for them, than to water down your message and try to shove it down uninterested people's throats.

I recommend that my nonprofit clients write a manifesto for their organizations. Sure, we all have "values statements" and "guiding principles" but they are often generic, basic, and full of jargon and insider-speak. A manifesto is designed to be a call-to-arms. It's purpose is to inspire. Your manifesto should serve as your content values statement, your brand voice, and a guide for your social media posts. It is a bold set of beliefs that challenge your audience to pick a side—Do you believe what we believe? Do you value what we value? Are you with us—or against us?

When writing your manifesto, ask:
- What do we want to change?
- What do we find unacceptable in this world?
- What are we fighting for?
- Who are we fighting for?
- What do we want people to feel when they encounter our work?
- Who are we doing this work for?

A manifesto articulates what the organization believes and stands for. It draws a line in the sand and invites people in, while letting others know that your mission and your work may not be for them. I know that to many nonprofits the thought of "turning people off" is terrifying. But the only way to build a thriving movement and a community of people who care enough to act on your behalf is to draw them in. Craft a message that speaks directly to those who will either benefit from your services or advocate for your cause (or both). *You cannot speak to and appeal to everyone*—you have to choose.

A great example of a powerful nonprofit manifesto comes from Planned Parenthood. The manifesto lays out their priorities, what they are fighting for, and describes a vision for the world they are seeking to create.

"We believe:

1. Our bodies are our own. If they are not, we cannot be truly equal.

2. Everyone deserves health care. It's a human right.

3. We must have the freedom to decide for ourselves whether and when to have children. This includes access to abortion. It's not up to politicians, corporations, pharmacists, college presidents, or insurers to decide.

4. Birth control is basic health care. We all deserve access.

5. We all deserve to be safe and free from sexual assault, harassment, and violence. That means consent.

6. We deserve economic equality. Equal pay and equal opportunity are essential to reach our full potential.

7. All people deserve healthy and safe pregnancies, births, and paid family and medical leave. We must support parents and all people who care for loved ones.

8. We reject racism, sexism, ableism, homophobia, and transphobia. We all deserve to live our lives freely and safely."

Even better, under Planned Parenthood's manifesto, they encourage like-minded fighters to join them in this movement, and to sign the digital manifesto by agreeing to this powerful statement: "My name is _____ and I am unstoppable."

Another example is the environmental organization Greenpeace. They created the Detox Fashion Manifesto to spread their belief that fashion shouldn't be toxic to the environment. The manifesto appeals to people interested in fashion and activism, and unites them in a common cause.

"We are a global movement of fashionistas, activists, designers and bloggers united by a belief that beautiful fashion shouldn't cause toxic pollution. We want the clothes we wear to be as stylish and authentic as we are. This is our Detox Fashion Manifesto:

1. We believe that brands and suppliers must act immediately to stop poisoning waterways around the world with hazardous chemicals.

2. We recognise that this will not happen overnight, and want brands and suppliers to be transparent about what chemicals they are releasing into the environment on the road toward toxic-free fashion. It is our water, we have a right to know.

3. We believe in rewarding and collaborating with honest and progressive suppliers and brands, and will encourage others to do the same."

Having a specific manifesto around a particular piece of your mission, like Greenpeace, is just as effective as creating a more general manifesto uniting people around your overall vision, like Planned Parenthood. Your nonprofit manifesto will look different and should encompass different beliefs. It may talk about how you have never and will never accept federal grant money, or how you protect client integrity at all costs, or how you believe in transparency and accessibility. Write it all down. Edit. Show it to board members, staff, volunteers, donors, and stakeholders for their ideas, feedback, and buy-in.

Nonprofit Social Media Blueprint: Write down at least three points that you would include in your nonprofit's manifesto. Look at the examples cited in this book for inspiration.

CHAPTER 4

Selection of Strategies

Strategies are general activities we need to carry out in order to reach our goal. The strategies are tailored to our target audience, to encourage them to take the action we seek. They are not specific tasks or platforms (that comes next), but rather ideas of how one could get to the goal. Strategies are always tailored to the identified target audience, to best encourage them to take the action we seek. If we are successful in systematically implementing our chosen strategies, then our goal will be in sight!

Let's go back to the list of common goals that nonprofits choose for their social media and online community building work. We will then come up with sample strategies that match each goal.

Goal	Strategies
(Example) To use social media to become an indispensable part of the community, so much so that even people that do not directly use our services and benefit from our programs would miss us if we were gone.	(Example) Establish trust and credibility with our stakeholders. Clearly demonstrate evidence of impact. Be seen as the local go-to resource around the issue.
(Example) To build an active and motivated online community ready and willing to support our work and advocate for our issue.	(Example) Share more inspiring stories of the people that we serve. Shed light on the complex issues that we tackle. Provide the community with resources such as a tool kit, videos, photos, stories.
(Example) To drive donations for our year-end fundraising campaign.	(Example) Collect, craft, and share stories that elicit an emotion so people will give. Make a compelling case for giving—why now, why this?

One way to think of this is to see the goal as the why, the audience as the who, the strategy as the what, and the action items and tasks (next chapter) as the when, where, and HOW. In Chapter 6, we will list out the tasks and tactics involved with each chosen strategy. I look at strategies more like overall projects we agree to take on to move ourselves towards success.

For example, if our goal is to become an indispensable part of the community, we need to commit to a strategy of creating and sharing social media content that establishes trust and credibility. The specific nuts and bolts of topics, types of content, social media cadence, and other logistical and content creation details will be tackled in the next two sections.

Nonprofit Social Media Blueprint: Brainstorm as many strategies as you can for each goal, with your staff, Board, or by yourself. Then whittle down your long list to three strategies for each goal. The goal is the "why" of the work and the strategies are the "what."

CHAPTER 5

Picking Platforms

In the final section of your Nonprofit Social Media Blueprint, you will select the best social media platforms that match with your chosen strategies. The platforms you employ function as the roads, bridges, and highways to get you to your destination. It's important that you make confident, informed decisions around the channels and platforms you choose, as well as the ones that you DO NOT choose. You will no doubt be forced to say "no thanks; not at this time" to many, many tempting and alluring platforms. Saying no right now does not mean no forever, but the ability to refrain from some platforms and prioritize others will prevent overwhelm and supercharge your focus and productivity.

It's not enough to have one overarching "digital plan" that covers all the tools, mobile apps, and social media platforms. There is no one size fits all in the digital space (not that there ever was, but even less so now). So instead of thinking about an all-encompassing "social media" strategy, you really need to adopt a Twitter strategy, and a Facebook strategy, and an Instagram strategy, and a LinkedIn strategy, and beyond. This is why it is crucial to get very clear on your capacity and what you can realistically add to your already-full plate. Evaluating and exploring certain platforms will allow you to jettison a bunch and keep a select few. This is a crucial part of the work of a savvy, work-smarter-not-harder nonprofit social media manager.

When selecting social media platforms, think of each as a separate country, with a distinct language, culture, etiquette, and inhabitants. Each network has unique properties, strengths, and weaknesses. For example, you wouldn't buy a guidebook for Germany if you were taking a trip to South Africa.

The good news is that you do NOT have to be everywhere at once—just the opposite! In fact, you may decide that you want to focus your marketing efforts solely on one or two social networks. Quality rules over quantity on social media, and consistency is the name of the game. There are no right or wrong answers here, just best practices that you can adapt for your individual organization and circumstances. It's entirely up to you where you focus your limited time and resources.

Should We Be On There?

So how do you know which platforms to choose for your nonprofit? Here is a quick assessment to use when evaluating individual platforms and apps:

- Is your target audience on this platform?
- Can you add value on this platform?

- Can you consistently create and share content that is designed for this specific channel; content that is not simply automated?

- Do you have the internal capacity and resources to respond to comments and questions, actively participate and not just "post and run"?

- Do you have the time to learn the unique language and best practices of a new platform?

- Can you analyze your work on this platform through analytics and insights, in order to improve?

For small nonprofits, setting up shop on fewer platforms may be best in the long run. My advice is to master one network, then move to another. The most important criteria to use when choosing social media networks is to go *where your audience spends the most time.* If you find that your donors and your stakeholders all love Twitter but your nonprofit is not actively using this channel, then you need to create a plan to reach them where they are, on their terms. But if you find that Twitter has no role to play in getting you to success, feel free to break up with the blue bird.

Ask yourself honestly: What is realistic for your nonprofit to manage? Consider the nine essential elements required in effectively managing a social media platform for marketing purposes:

1. Frequent, consistent creation of unique content that serves a purpose.

2. Finding and curating good content to share that is relevant to your audience.

3. Monitoring topics and hashtags to stay tuned to what is trending and on people's minds.

4. Regularly commenting on others' content.
5. Answering questions from your audience and direct messages in a timely fashion.
6. Acknowledging community members that share your content and comment.
7. Keeping track of what has been shared.
8. Measuring what works and doing more of it.
9. Analysis and improvement.

When evaluating and choosing platforms, remember that social media is unpredictable! You have zero control over how these businesses (and they are all businesses) operate, their choices, and their priorities. Social media marketing is big money, and many of these platforms change with the shifting winds, or at the will of the public, the government, or the shareholders.

Why do billions of people use social media on a daily basis? Spoiler alert—it is NOT to view solicitations, appeals, promotions, and ads. Snapchat and Murphy Research conducted a study of more than 1,000 social media users, between the ages of 13-44, to learn more about the social apps they use and why they use them.

According to this report, the three most popular reasons that people use social media are:

1. To talk to their friends.
2. To connect with their family.
3. To share photos and videos.

Different platforms unsurprisingly have different uses, with Twitter cited as a place to "learn about topics of interest" and "share views and opinions on topics" and Facebook to "learn about events."

Let's take as an example the IRS' new Instagram Strategy. Yes, the IRS is on Instagram, and it's one of the more vibrant accounts on there! The department has a stated goal of getting their message out to different audiences and reaching younger taxpayers, millennials especially. In an interview, their social media lead said that "It's a matter of meeting the taxpayers where they are." Their goal is to spread useful information to help people get ready for the upcoming tax season and to prevent common tax scams.

Based purely on current demographic evidence, if your want to target a younger demographic, you need to at least explore using YouTube and Snapchat. If you want to reach journalists and thought leaders, you should explore Twitter. Want to run peer-to-peer fundraising campaigns? Facebook is the place to be. LinkedIn is great to publish a blog and to connect with professional colleagues and potential corporate partners.

As you have probably figured out, accomplishing your goals will undoubtedly require offline tactics combined with other digital strategies, like email newsletters, website overhauls, and more. In the realm of digital marketing, you get out what you put in, depending on how you use the tools and to what purpose. You can use a hammer to build a city or to hang a picture (and each is a valuable use to a specific set of people).

I never recommend that nonprofits eliminate analog tactics—direct mail, phone calls, coffees, events, and the like—if they are working. Social media should augment and amplify the other work that you are doing. However, for the purposes of this section and this book, we will focus on social media tactics.

Nonprofit Social Media Blueprint: Choose three potential social media channels to evaluate and answer the yes or no questions on the chart.

Quick Primer on Six Popular Social Media Platforms

Facebook

Facebook is now used by two billion people, and it's pretty mind-blowing how in just one decade the most vilified and celebrated social network has completely changed how humans across the world communicate. People are often ostracized for NOT using Facebook, because it's better for the individual user if all of their friends, family, favorite brands, and pet causes are on there. Can you think of any other business or product with such a powerful social pull to join and to comply?

What you need to know: Facebook's ubiquity among all age groups and demographics, combined with a very low barrier to entry, had most of us using it in our personal lives years before we discovered it's potential for marketing. It remains the most popular social network used by nonprofits because it has the widest appeal. In general: 68% of U.S. adults use Facebook.

Facebook's most recent pivot towards privacy will undoubtedly have huge implications for marketers, most of which have yet to be fully realized.

Facebook Business Pages

Nonprofits on Facebook should set up an official Business Page rather than a Profile. The Page is their public-facing presence on Facebook, where they can share updates, photos, videos, stories, create events, and purchase ads.

Strengths: Facebook is the most-widely used of the major social media platforms, and its user base is most broadly representative of the population as a whole. Their ad targeting features are incredibly useful when used strategically.

Weaknesses: Getting engagement on Facebook is difficult, and organic reach has plummeted in recent months.

Best content: Live streaming video is the dominant content on the site. Native videos (videos posted inside the platform, rather than outside links) are the second best type of content for Facebook.

Facebook Groups

Facebook Groups can be a great way to engage a select group of people around a specific topic or issue. They can be linked to an official nonprofit Facebook Page.

Strengths: Facebook Groups get more engagement than Pages and tend to grow more quickly.

Weaknesses: The most successful Groups frown on too much traditional promotion, and can be time-consuming to manage and moderate.

Best content: Live streaming video inside the Group, polls, and posts that ask questions and encourage discussion and debate.

Facebook Fundraising Tools

Individuals and Facebook Business Pages can set up Facebook Fundraisers to raise money for your nonprofit. If you are a 501c3 and have an EIN number, you can register for Facebook Payments to receive these donations. There are no fees associated with fundraising on Facebook, if you are officially registered as a 501c3 nonprofit with the platform.

Strengths: Facebook Fundraisers are incredibly easy to set up and start using. Users can set up a Fundraiser and invite their network to join them with just a few clicks. If the nonprofit is set up with Facebook Payments, donations can be collected in just two simple clicks, making it incredibly easy for the donor. Facebook eliminated fees to the Fundraisers.

Weaknesses: The nonprofit gets little to no information on the donors who give through the platform.

Best content: The most successful Facebook Fundraisers feature a personal story of the person raising the money and a personalized appeal to friends, family, and colleagues, encouraging them to participate.

Answer these questions when evaluating:	Facebook:
Is your target audience on this platform?	
Can you add value on this platform through consistent sharing of unique, helpful content designed for your audience?	
Can you consistently create and share content that is designed for this specific channel; content that is not simply automated?	
Do you have the internal capacity and resources to respond to comments and questions, actively participate and not just "post and run"?	
Do you have the time to learn the unique language and best practices of a new platform?	
Can you analyze your work on this platform through analytics and insights, in order to improve?	

If you did not answer yes for at least three of the six questions, your organization may not be ready to use this particular social media platform.

Twitter

Twitter is a great tool for nonprofits looking to connect with influencers, bloggers, journalists, and thought leaders. Twitter is most effective for nonprofits working on time-sensitive, urgent issues that need to activate large groups with a moments notice, or for groups that require having their finger on the pulse of industry news and announcements. Of U.S. adults, 24% use Twitter.

What you need to know: Chances are high that if you are a small, locally-based nonprofit only looking to push out promotional messages about your events and fundraisers, Twitter is not the ideal medium. This social network undoubtedly requires the most time and energy of all the social media platforms, in order to get real results. Between dealing with trolls and people who want to argue with your point of view to keeping up with the constant firehose of information, it can be overwhelming and prohibitively exhausting for a small nonprofit.

Twitter account (there is no differentiation between a Business account and a personal account)

Twitter works like the fast-paced newsroom of the internet. People use Twitter to comment on news and current events, to share helpful resources and articles, and to engage with friends and colleagues.

Strengths: Twitter is a powerful search engine to discover what people are talking about and to find conversations around issues and causes. Using hashtags on the site and tagging specific accounts can get nonprofits more exposure and increase visibility.

Weaknesses: Twitter is time-consuming and requires a lot of give and take. Accounts need to actively participate frequently, share valuable content, and respond to retweets and questions in a timely manner.

Best content: Videos and posts with visuals work best on Twitter. Using hashtags and tagging relevant accounts works to get your tweets seen by more people.

Answer these questions when evaluating:	Twitter:
Is your target audience on this platform?	
Can you add value on this platform through consistent sharing of unique, helpful content designed for your audience?	
Can you consistently create and share content that is designed for this specific channel; content that is not simply automated?	
Do you have the internal capacity and resources to respond to comments and questions, actively participate and not just "post and run"?	
Do you have the time to learn the unique language and best practices of a new platform?	
Can you analyze your work on this platform through analytics and insights, in order to improve?	

If you did not answer yes for at least three of the six questions, your organization may not be ready to use this particular social media platform.

Instagram

Right now, I am loving Instagram for nonprofits! As of this writing, Instagram is one of the only social media platforms experiencing growth instead of stagnation or decline. People love it's clean aesthetic, how it isn't cluttered with links and articles and a lot of back and forth debate, like Facebook or Twitter.

What you need to know: If you want to target a younger demographic, Instagram could be for you, with 59% of online adults aged 18-29 active on the network. More than 500 million people have Instagram accounts, more than 300 million of which use it daily. Another key characteristic that differentiates Instagram from social media stalwarts Facebook or Twitter is the way in which people use it. Instagrammers frequently check the site, often several times a day, and engage with posts at a much higher rate than other social networks.

Instagram Business Account

Instagram is a visual social media platform where people and brands post eye-catching photos and videos. Instagram Stories is a feature that lets users post photos and videos that vanish after 24 hours and do not appear in your profile grid or the main Instagram feed.

Strengths: Instagram is one of the fastest growing social media platforms, and the platform with the highest percentage of engagement. People go to Instagram to like photos and comment on photos, and users visit the site more frequently than other platforms. It's most popular feature, Instagram Stories, are watched and created by over 500 million people daily.

Weaknesses: The Instagram feed is crowded with tons of great (and not-so-great) photos and videos, and it can be hard to cut through the clutter. Success on Instagram means creating eye-catching visuals, writing engaging captions, and using hashtags strategically.

Best content: Photos with text overlay, beautiful graphics, landscape shots, and photos of people. A beautiful, colorful, interesting photo always wins on Instagram.

Answer these questions when evaluating:	Instagram:
Is your target audience on this platform?	
Can you add value on this platform through consistent sharing of unique, helpful content designed for your audience?	
Can you consistently create and share content that is designed for this specific channel; content that is not simply automated?	
Do you have the internal capacity and resources to respond to comments and questions, actively participate and not just "post and run"?	
Do you have the time to learn the unique language and best practices of a new platform?	
Can you analyze your work on this platform through analytics and insights, in order to improve?	

If you did not answer yes for at least three of the six questions, your organization may not be ready to use this particular social media platform

YouTube

YouTube is a free video sharing service where users can create their own profile, upload videos, watch, like and comment on other videos. Of U.S. adults, 73% use YouTube.

Strengths: YouTube is the #2 search engine in the world, owned by the largest search engine, Google. Users go to the site specifically to discover and watch videos. Nonprofits can sign up for a free account and receive special features. They recently announced a new suite of Giving Tools to make it much easier and more seamless to give money on the platform, similar to the Facebook donate button and Facebook birthday fundraisers. When people visit YouTube they tend to stay there longer and spend more time than other social media sites, which gives an advantage to nonprofits creating and leveraging the power of video and storytelling on the site.

Weaknesses: It is a very crowded place, and hard to get visibility without paying for ads. To be successful on YouTube you must spend time on the title of the video, the caption, and the promotion.

Best content: A branded channel that consistently posts valuable videos works best.

Answer these questions when evaluating:	YouTube:
Is your target audience on this platform?	
Can you add value on this platform through consistent sharing of unique, helpful content designed for your audience?	
Can you consistently create and share content that is designed for this specific channel; content that is not simply automated?	

Do you have the internal capacity and resources to respond to comments and questions, actively participate and not just "post and run"?	
Do you have the time to learn the unique language and best practices of a new platform?	
Can you analyze your work on this platform through analytics and insights, in order to improve?	

If you did not answer yes for at least three of the six questions, your organization may not be ready to use this particular social media platform.

LinkedIn

LinkedIn is the wildly underestimated dark horse of the social media stable. Data shows that LinkedIn is growing steadily—two professionals join every second, and as of this writing, 154 million Americans have profiles. If your nonprofit is looking to connect with higher income populations, 50% of Americans with a college degree use LinkedIn, and 45% of users are in "upper management" of some kind.

With the release of several new features, including live video streaming capability and voice messaging, LinkedIn shouldn't be ignored when nonprofits plan their Social Media Roadmap. According to the site, over 10 million users have indicated interest in skill-based volunteering, board service, or mentoring opportunities. Without the bluster of Twitter or the emotion of Facebook, LinkedIn is a great place to find donor and Board prospects, make professional connections, and grow your nonprofit's community of business professionals.

LinkedIn Personal Profile: LinkedIn is a professional networking platform, where individuals can create profiles detailing their professional credentials.

LinkedIn Company Page: Brands and organizations can create Company Pages to post jobs and showcase news and announcements.

Strengths: LinkedIn is used by professionals of all ages, and has a more formal vibe than the other social networks. People go to LinkedIn to build their careers, network, and market their businesses and services.

Weaknesses: This platform can be less engaging than the others, and people do not use LinkedIn as much or spend as much aimless, scrolling time on it as the other popular social media sites.

Best content: Video works best to stand out.

Answer these questions when evaluating:	LinkedIn:
Is your target audience on this platform?	
Can you add value on this platform through consistent sharing of unique, helpful content designed for your audience?	
Can you consistently create and share content that is designed for this specific channel; content that is not simply automated?	
Do you have the internal capacity and resources to respond to comments and questions, actively participate and not just "post and run"?	

Do you have the time to learn the unique language and best practices of a new platform?	
Can you analyze your work on this platform through analytics and insights, in order to improve?	

If you did not answer yes for at least three of the six questions, your organization may not be ready to use this particular social media platform.

Pinterest

Often seen as just a place to plan a party or to completely redesign your bedroom, Pinterest use remains steady with 250 million active monthly users. Of users, 81% are female (40% of new sign-ups to the site are men) and as a general trend, women at virtually every income level are most likely to give to causes they care about. Not only that, when women find a nonprofit they click with, they give more and they are more loyal.

My favorite characteristic of Pinterest is that it represents our aspirations, not just our in-the-moment experiences. It's also transactional, not relational like Facebook or Instagram. What we pin reflects what we covet, what moves us, what we desire, and who we want to be. Pinterest works much more like a vision board, rather than an off-the-cuff, in-the-moment statement of what we are eating or where we are hanging out.

Pinterest Business Account

Pinterest is a visual platform, composed of pins and pin boards. Users save pins to specific pin boards which can be public or private, and are organized around specific topics or ideas. Of U.S. adults, 29% use Pinterest.

Strengths: People go to Pinterest to discover new things, and to collect ideas to use in the future. This platform is very aspirational—it's all about the future, rather than the present (i.e. this is what I'm eating right now, this is the place I am in right now).

Weaknesses: You have to create images that work well for Pinterest, and you need to be active on the site to get traction.

Best content: Long, vertical images work best.

Answer these questions when evaluating:	Pinterest:
Is your target audience on this platform?	
Can you add value on this platform through consistent sharing of unique, helpful content designed for your audience?	
Can you consistently create and share content that is designed for this specific channel; content that is not simply automated?	
Do you have the internal capacity and resources to respond to comments and questions, actively participate and not just "post and run"?	
Do you have the time to learn the unique language and best practices of a new platform?	
Can you analyze your work on this platform through analytics and insights, in order to improve?	

If you did not answer yes for at least three of the six questions, your organization may not be ready to use this particular social media platform.

Nonprofit Social Media Blueprint: Choose three potential social media channels to evaluate and answer the yes or no questions on the worksheet. Then decide if you want to pursue all three platforms, two, or just one of them.

CHAPTER 6

Matching Up Tasks

In Chapter 4, you selected the main strategies required to accomplish your goal, and in Chapter 5, you evaluated and prioritized the specific social media platforms to carry out your strategies. Congratulations!! Now you are ready to write down the fun stuff—the daily, weekly, and monthly tasks that go into making all of this a reality.

You may have noticed that strategies tend to be broad and vague—behavior changes that you seek in your audience, feelings that you need to inspire, overall initiatives and projects. Strategies are the what of your social media plan—nonprofits know what they need to do on social media, but they may not know how.

Simply writing down "Establish trust with our donors" or "Be seen as the local go-to resource" on your To Do list won't cut it. We have to break down the strategies even further into specific tasks.

Your tasks should directly match up with your strategies. Tasks are where the rubber meets the road—the action steps required to move the needle on the strategies. Each strategy will have different tasks that work best (some will overlap). Tasks and tools may come and go, some will falter and fail, and some will get replaced over time. But your goal, audience, message, and strategies that you laid out in your Nonprofit Social Media Blueprint will hold fast.

Some examples of tasks that match with the selected nonprofit social media strategies and platforms:

Strategies	Platforms	Tasks
(Example) Establish trust and credibility with our stakeholders. Clearly demonstrate evidence of impact. Be seen as the local go-to resource around the issue.	Facebook, Instagram, YouTube	Share one video each week with news focused on the issue, adding in our unique perspective and viewpoint.
(Example) Share more inspiring stories of the people that we serve. Shed light on the complex issues that we tackle. Provide the community with resources such as a tool kit, videos, photos, stories.	Facebook, LinkedIn, Instagram	Create a weekly video series with the Executive Director on a relevant topic or question related to our cause. Address FAQs about our work in a series of short videos on Facebook. Share testimonials on Instagram.

(Example) Collect, craft, and share stories that elicit an emotion so people will give. Make a compelling case for giving—why now, why this?	Facebook, Instagram, YouTube	Share Instagram Stories once per week from the field. Hold a digital storytelling training for staff and board members. Invest in a video series depicting transformational client stories.

As you can see, the more strategies and platforms you select, the greater the task list becomes. I recommend limiting the number of tasks to increase your focus and prevent overwhelm and burnout.

After you list out the tasks that you want to embark on, estimate how much time each one will take. Many of the tasks you select can be carried out for free, but you also need to estimate if any budget will be required—such as video production, editing software, stock photography purchases, and the like.

Tasks	Time Estimate (Per Task)	Budget
Share one video each week with news focused on the issue, adding in our unique perspective and viewpoint.	Two hours to research and prepare the video content, 30 minutes to shoot the video, One hour to edit	Smartphone app for editing video; microphone; extra lighting; tripod for smartphone

Create a weekly video series with the Executive Director on a relevant topic or question related to our cause. Address FAQs about our work in a series of short posts with photos. Share testimonials on Instagram.	Two hours to prepare questions and set up equipment to film, one hour to promote the video series each week Two hours to create and write the posts, one hour to find accompanying photos Two hours to collect the stories, one hour to get photos to go with them	Facebook Ads to boost the video series, equipment for shooting the video on a smartphone or laptop High quality stock photography (there are many free sites as well, or you can use your own photos)
Share Instagram Stories once per week from the field. Hold a digital storytelling training for staff and board members. Invest in a video series depicting transformational client stories.	10 minutes per day to create and share Stories live from the field Two hours to find a consultant, three hours for the training, three hours of follow up with the staff 10 hours of work with a video production company (depending on the number of videos)	No budget needed Consultant to provide the training and materials Video production company to create a series of high-end videos

Nonprofit Social Media Blueprint: Brainstorm as many tasks as you can for each strategy and platform, with your staff, Board,

or by yourself. Then choose two or three tasks, based on the time commitment and estimated budget, and what you know you can accomplish realistically.

CHAPTER 7

Growing an Organizational Culture that Embraces Social Media

You have great ideas about how to use social media to amplify your cause, and you can't wait to share them with your boss. You take screenshots of innovative campaigns, read blogs, and do the legwork to stay up-to-date on social media trends and best practices.

Then you approach your Board or your boss with potential social media initiatives, and they say no, let's just keep things the way they are. Status quo all the way. (Sigh.)

No amount of social media savvy will matter if the rest of the staff is apathetic, uninterested, or worse, resistant to the change you wish to make. In this chapter, we will review the best ways to get buy-in from your entire organization and how to create a Social Media Task Force of people to help with the ideas and the work.

In this chapter I outline the four tasks that will help you on your quest to secure buy-in and to build a culture that understands and embraces community building on social media.

1. Address the Social Media Skeptics in your organization (with empathy).
2. Create internal and external (public-facing) social media policies.
3. Conduct workshops and trainings on social media, either formally with an outside consultant or informally during internal meetings, or with lunch and learns.
4. Empower your co-workers to participate in the process by creating a Social Media Task Force.

Step 1: Address the Skeptics.

In order to build a new culture, we have to understand what may be holding the organization back from embracing social media and digital marketing. We need to understand the roadblocks to create a plan to overcome them.

In my business I meet a lot of people with a lot of interesting opinions about social media. These opinions range from "It's fantastic! I use it every day!" to "I don't get it but I'm willing to learn" to "I hate it and I think it's the downfall of society." People certainly have the right to their opinion. If someone absolutely loathes the internet and all that it represents, I won't waste my time discussing all the revolutionary and important uses for it. (Thankfully, these people are in the minority.)

The social media converts and die-hards are fun to talk to because we are usually on the same page and have some ideas to bounce off of each other. The group of people that really challenges me is the skeptics. Skepticism and apprehension are driven by fear, and in this case, the fear of social media is the fear of the unknown or the fear of that which you cannot control.

Social Media Skeptics can be individuals that have heard of social media and are afraid to start using it, or people that are dabbling in social media but not sure how to proceed in a strategic way to market their causes. They can be intrigued by the platforms personally, but not entirely convinced of the usefulness or relevance to them or their work.

In my experience, there are three types of Social Media Skeptics:

- The Emotional Skeptic: The Emotional Skeptic is afraid of everyone knowing the details of their private life. They are primarily worried about privacy issues and fear that their information will be stolen, copied or otherwise misused.

- The Logical Skeptic: The Logical Skeptic feels that social media is an unproven medium. They need to see immediate ROI (return on investment) on their marketing strategies, and are not sure that social media marketing will help their business.

- The Overwhelmed Skeptic: The Overwhelmed Skeptic is just that—overwhelmed! They are weighed down by the sheer amount of information out there, and believe that they have no time to learn how to manage social media accounts.

So what to do when you encounter a Social Media Skeptic?

1. Figure out which type they fit into, and inquire about their concerns. People like to be listened to and responded to in a genuine, caring way. Trying something new is scary, and people don't like to be rushed.

2. Show them the data. Explain that people of all ages use social media. Nonprofits now have to engage and interact with five distinct generations of supporters. Social media participation crosses the majority of these five generations.

3. Show Skeptics concrete ways in which social media can be useful. I find compelling examples of social media in action—businesses using it to address customer service concerns, individuals using it to connect to issues they care about, nonprofits using it to fundraise and to find volunteers. Have a Pinterest board ready to go with examples of innovative and interesting social media campaigns, or even just screenshots from posts that you like. Many Skeptics still think that social media is just a bunch of people posting what they had for lunch that day.

4. Make it simple and go slowly. Explain it in layman's terms. When I first meet with someone, I don't immediately throw around words like "retweet," "hashtag," "check-in" and "analytics". I feel out the situation and the individual's comfort level and skill, and go from there. I am careful not to act patronizing or belittling, and I certainly don't force my opinions on anyone—who would that benefit? Remember the old tale of the rabbit and the tortoise: Slowly and surely wins the race.

5. Address the elephant in the room. Can social media really provide ROI (return on investment) for the nonprofit? If you have a social media program running, share the data and the stats, and show progress towards results and a plan to move forward. If not, explain to your supervisor that you will regularly evaluate and measure what you are doing online in order to best iterate and improve.

Step 2: Create social media policies for your organization.

People that are skeptical of social media may be concerned that opening up this can of worms at your nonprofit will create conflicts of interest, policy breaches, and more messy legal situations. Work to create clear and concise policies that empower and educate all staff and volunteers.

Some nonprofit supervisors want to turn a blind eye or simply forbid everyone from using Facebook at work. This is counterproductive and in my opinion, pointless. A better idea is to provide staff and volunteers with helpful guidelines as to what is acceptable and what is discouraged.

These guidelines would include examples of what is ok to share online, and what is not ideal. Social Media Policy trainings are the perfect teachable moment for younger people in the office who may not be accustomed to censoring themselves online in any way, and will also create security for others who may not be sure where the boundaries are on social media.

Internal Social Media Policies

Internal social media policies should accomplish two objectives:

1. Spell out clearly what kind of behaviors are discouraged on social media by staff, volunteers, and anyone else who represents the organization; and

2. Specify what types of behaviors are encouraged or even required by this group.

Look at your current organizational policies for employees and volunteers if you have a handbook or other materials used during orientations or trainings. You may be surprised what your current staff and volunteers DON'T know about the policies you already have in place on paper, but may not be readily enforced.

Your organization needs to ensure that everyone is on the same page about the following questions:

- What organization-related information should be always confidential and why? Is the safety of the staff and clients at stake if there is a confidentiality breach? Will you lose funding? Will you lose integrity and lose the trust of the community?

- What do breaches of confidentiality look like? Give examples, either from real life or made up. Show offline and online examples.

- What are the individual consequences for ignoring these policies? What will happen? Will they get fired? Unpaid leave?

- Do you allow and encourage staff to identify themselves as employees on their social networks and on official social media channels?

- Are staff and volunteers required to participate in social media work by sharing photos, videos, stories, and other content with the marketing manager?

A nonprofit should do its best to encourage an open, transparent culture of education and empowerment around social media, not one of fear, accusations, and finger-pointing. Model good behaviors of productive sharing and positive participation on social media.

External Social Media Policies

It is also vital for a nonprofit to have disclaimers or brief statements on their social media accounts that explain what is encouraged and what could get someone removed. If there is no place to add this policy to your bio on a particular social media site, make sure this public-facing policy resides somewhere on your website.

When formulating your social media policies, questions to address include:

- What will you encourage people to post on your nonprofit's Facebook page, and what is inappropriate to share there?

- Will you let your clients interact in your online communities as long as they are anonymous? Jayne Cravens, TechSoup's Community Forum Manager, recommends: "The best way to protect confidentiality is to think about humans as much as, if not more, than the technology."

External policies should be kept simple, but be clear, concise, and unambiguous. This way, if you remove a comment or ban a person from your social media accounts, you can refer back to your policy, your online community knows what to expect, and if they violate the policy you can assure them that they are not being arbitrarily targeted.

Sample language from a Facebook policy I created with my client Beverly Bootstraps:

Welcome to the official Facebook fan page for Beverly Bootstraps Community Services, Inc.! Here we will share news about our programs to provide critical resources to families and individuals so that they may reach self-sufficiency. We will also post updates about events, photos, videos, interesting stories and news articles.

We want to keep our Facebook page an open forum, but we are also a "family friendly" page, so please keep comments and wall posts clean. We want you to tell us what's on your mind, but if it falls into any of the categories below, we want to let you know beforehand that we will have to remove it:

    — *We do not allow graphic, obscene, explicit or racial comments or submissions nor do we allow comments that are abusive, hateful or intended to defame anyone or any organization.*

    — *We do not allow third party solicitations or advertisements. This includes promotion or endorsement of any financial, commercial or non-governmental agency. Similarly, we do not allow attempts to defame or defraud any financial, commercial or non-governmental agency.*

    — *We do not allow comments that support or encourage illegal activity.*

    Also, the appearance of external links on this page does not constitute an official endorsement on behalf of Beverly Bootstraps—it just might be something we found interesting and wanted to share!

    Whew! Now that all THAT is out of the way, let's get to know each other. Post, share and tell us what you'd like to see more of from Beverly Bootstraps!

Examples of internal and external social media policies for nonprofits can be found at the book resource site: www.jcsocial-marketing.com/socialmediabook.

Step 3. Formal and informal trainings on social media and nonprofit digital

Bringing in outside experts for formal training sessions, as well as holding casual discussions around social media and nonprofit digital work, can help break down myths and misconceptions and encourage everyone to contribute.

People that work for or volunteer with your nonprofit already have social media accounts of some form or another—you can bet on that. But personal use of social media is vastly different than using it to advocate for your mission and amplifying your impact. The key is getting staff to truly understand the value of these platforms for marketing your nonprofit's programs, services, and mission.

In order to get respect for your job, your co-workers need to appreciate just how much work it takes to build an online community. Explain that getting results on social media is nuanced and complex, and involves a combination of strategy, learning, research, creativity, experimentation, design, listening, and measurement.

I recommend organizing a series of short "lunch and learns" for interested staff and volunteers on various social media topics or platforms. The goal is not to tell people the "right" or "wrong" way to do things, but to encourage discussion, discovery, and debate around these topics.

Here are some topic ideas to get you started:

- Digital Communications 101—how all staff and volunteers represent the nonprofit, even on personal accounts;
- What's a Hashtag? and Other Common Social Media Questions
- Social Media Pros and Cons—the strengths and weaknesses of the major platforms along with some examples of how nonprofits leverage digital to expand their reach
- Open discussion: What is appropriate to share and what is not on Facebook, LinkedIn, Twitter, personal blogs, etc.? Is fundraising ok? Promoting events? Sharing articles relating to the nonprofit cause? Advocacy?
- Campaign Planning: What is involved in planning a social media campaign? Is identifying your location or "checking in" ok? (Think Facebook, Instagram, and Foursquare.)

Along with formal professional development and trainings, bake social media work into all organizational gatherings. Take ten minutes at each staff meeting and show everyone your editorial calendar and list of content ideas. Instead of just "reporting out," ask for direct feedback and take questions. Work towards a culture where you are the driver of the social media train, but everyone feels that their ideas are heard. They will be much more likely to share stories and other content ideas with you if they know you respect them.

I believe that the marketing department (even if it's just one person) should have an open-door policy. Other staff members will surely have questions or thoughts that they may not want to bring up during a group discussion, and they need to know they can look to you for information and advice in the social media realm.

Your co-workers can also serve as a wealth of new, creative ideas on how best to use these channels. Hold weekly office hours for staff to come in and discuss social media and digital marketing. Encourage them to send you their ideas and examples of nonprofit social media campaigns that they like or that inspire them.

Step 4: Create a Social Media Task Force

In addition to having an open mind and an open door for staff and others to share their ideas and feedback with you, I recommend creating a team of digital leaders to serve as a Social Media Task Force. The Task Force can share details of the work at organization meetings and gatherings, and can also help you advocate for more staff, budget, or even just more respect.

Sample tasks of the Social Media Task Force include:

- Meet bi-monthly to review website, email, social media channels.

- Collect and craft stories about the work.
- Refer back to the Social Media Roadmap as the guiding document.
- Evaluate policies and procedures for social media internally and externally.
- Conduct training for staff and volunteers.
- Brainstorm content ideas.

How you design the Task Force is up to you, but make sure to recruit people who are excited and passionate about the work and about digital technology to participate. Here's a sample Social Media Task Force member job description that you can use or modify:

Members will actively participate in forming and carrying out the social media strategy of the organization. They will attend meetings, bring ideas and creative energy to the group, and implement strategies as assigned, including engaging with the organization on social media platforms, promoting the social media accounts of the organization and inviting others to become involved.

Step 5: Advocate for Your Work

We know that nonprofit staff are busy, overwhelmed, and under-paid. In many nonprofits, hard-working people are putting their heads down and doing the work each and every day, for very little recognition and accolades, with little to no collaboration throughout the organization. For program staff and marketing staff alike, it's hard to feel appreciated by your co-workers if they don't understand what you do or why you do it.

Despite the proliferation of digital communication and social media in our daily lives, nonprofits still often draw distinct silos between marketing, development, and program staff in a way that limits communication and understanding. Co-workers may want to work together, but they don't know how to speak the same language, and they are often forced to view each other as competition for limited resources.

Often seen as a "nice-to-have" and not a "must-have" department, the reality is that marketing is one of the first departments to get their budget slashed, especially in small nonprofits. With the relentless and misguided focus on nonprofit overhead and so-called nonprofit "efficiency," it's hard to advocate for anything except direct program costs. Social media work often gets haphazardly added to an already overloaded job description without much thought as to the time and tasks involved.

To nonprofit marketers and social media managers, the problem is clear. Without marketing, potential supporters, volunteers, and advocates will not be made aware of the work. They won't be drawn in, led on a journey, educated, informed, and inspired to get involved.

This is true for staff members as well. We need to market our ideas and advocate for our work within our organizations, not just externally. We need to dismantle silos and address myths and misconceptions about digital marketing, social media, and online community building.

The mistake that many nonprofits make is to get one sole individual to be in charge of their social media channels, either an intern or a staff person. Often they give them the login information and then banish them to a remote office, or force them to work virtually. The reality is that to build an online community, social media managers need input from all aspects of the organization.

Marketing and fundraising are a piece of everyone's job. When I go into my local coffee shop, the barista greets me with a smile. When I visit the library, if the librarian or person at the front desk is surly or unfriendly, that reflects back on the entire organization.

As nonprofit marketers we know this. We have to continually have conversations with program officers, administrators, receptionists, people on the front lines, to help them understand this.

At the end of the day, don't let fear be the default. Allison Fine, co-author with Beth Kanter of the book, *The Networked Nonprofit: Connecting with Social Media to Drive Change*, writes: "It's easy to look for reasons not to do something, and we have been acculturated to think of that as smart management. But the risk of not becoming more social is too great to let fear continue to be the default setting for our organizations."

Nonprofit Social Media Blueprint: List two tactics that you are going to use to help co-workers and supervisors at your nonprofit understand and embrace the work that goes into a social media plan.

Part Two

CAPTIVATE

"The web has made kicking ass easier to achieve, and mediocrity harder to sustain. Mediocrity now howls in protest."
—Hugh MacLeod

What you need to complete this section:
- A copy of the Nonprofit Social Media Blueprint—
download it at www.jcsocialmarketing.com/
socialmediabook

Introduction

Congratulations! You successfully completed the first 30 days of activities in this book! Or maybe you skipped ahead because you got curious as to what comes next. Either way, you are moving right along on your journey to improve and rejuvenate your social media work at your nonprofit. You now have the basic infrastructure needed to build the rest of your Social Media Blueprint.

To review, in the last section we identified:

- Your goal—what you hope to achieve for your nonprofit on social media.
- Your audience—who you need to connect with and mobilize.
- Your message—the overarching, unifying call to action.
- Your strategies—the change in behavior and attitudes that you are seeking.
- Your platforms—where you will build your movement and inspire your target audience.
- Your tasks—the action items you need to carry out to make it all happen.

It's no small feat to accomplish the big picture work of the first section, and it definitely sets you up for social media success. During the next 30 days, we focus our efforts on collecting and crafting the best kinds of social media content—content that will captivate your audience and get them to not only pay attention, but motivate them to take action.

If the first 30 days were spent building the framework for your social media house, the next 30 are spent decorating it and filling it with furniture. In this section, we review the six pillars of a wildly successful nonprofit social media content strategy and choose the most relevant and effective content buckets for your nonprofit. We will also review several of the most common social media challenges faced by nonprofits, large and small, and the solutions we can employ to move us forward.

CHAPTER 8

The Six Pillars of Compelling Social Media Content for Nonprofits

Engagement is the currency that runs social media. The word engagement means different things on each of the big social networks—likes, comments, shares, retweets, re-pins, link clicks, Story comments, direct messages, etc. When a supporter takes an action, no matter how small, on your social media content, the platform takes note.

Without engagement, the social network algorithms that scan your accounts and others will "downvote" your posts, thinking that they are undesirable and irrelevant to your audience. In their never-ending rush to show interesting, relevant content to their users, and thus keep them on the site longer, social media algorithms determine in a split second what's interesting and what's not. Engagement and reach are very different metrics. If your social media content doesn't get any interaction, your efforts will fall flat, no matter how many ads you purchase or how many eyeballs see your post in their feeds.

The 90-9-1 Rule

The 90-9-1 Rule for Participation Inequality in Social Media and Online Communities is the result of a study conducted by Jakob Nielsen in 2006. It shows that in the majority of online communities on social networks:

- 90% of people are "lurkers"—passive consumers of content. This means they read, they look, they watch, but they do not contribute anything themselves.

- 9% of people contribute "somewhat" or "infrequently" to the online community, usually in the form of liking, commenting, or sharing.

- Only 1% of the online community members are "active" participants, creating their own content for the community, and they account for most of the contributions and posts.

Whether or not the 90-9-1 rule holds fast for your nonprofit and your audience is worth exploring. It's important to have realistic expectations in your social media work, as recent studies have shown that the vast majority of people are in fact lurkers—maybe not 90%, but a large percentage. Focus most of your energy on the members of your online community who are active participants, but don't ignore the rest of the users.

While you may never move the majority of your social media "lurkers" over to the 1% of your actively engaged online community, the goal should be moving the needle by growing your numbers and steadily increasing engagement over time.

I designed the Six Pillars of social media content with engagement at the forefront, to get you to move more of your lurkers into the "active participants" column. Many nonprofits think that simply telling people what they do is enough to succeed on social media. It's not. Simply giving people information, data, and warm fuzzies does not translate into people taking action.

The Six Pillars are also intended to help you attract and retain more of your online community members, by consistently providing value to their lives and giving them real reasons to continue to follow you. Beyond simply getting likes, your social media content should be focused on building an online community proud to be supporting you, and one that will go to bat for you when asked.

CHAPTER 9

Pillar One—
Content that Grabs Attention

Facebook marketing expert Mari Smith says that the number one goal on social media should be to make content that is "thumb stopping." This refers to the way that we scroll through our social media feeds on our smartphones, with our thumbs. When creating content, always ask yourself: What would make someone stop scrolling and pay attention?

Think about your own media consumption habits in the "distraction economy." In my world, I often have 10 or more Google Chrome tabs open, my phone right next to me, email inbox open, and music or news playing in the background. Despite numerous research studies showing the counterproductive nature of multi-tasking, we all do it—and with the proliferation of smart-phones, smart watches, and smart devices in our households and cars, even more so.

If your post doesn't catch my eye while I am perusing the latest photos of my friend's vacation on Facebook, engaging in a Twitter exchange about politics, or while stalking the latest Instagram posts from my favorite celebrities, then you are out of luck.

5 Ways to Grab Attention with Your Social Media Content

1. Incorporate eye-catching visuals.

Data and research repeatedly show that videos work best to capture attention, due to the eye-catching nature of movement. Colorful photos also catch the eye and draw people in. Whether you use videos, photos, or graphics that you design yourself using free tools like Canva or Adobe Spark, including a visual with every post on social media is mandatory. To see the examples mentioned here and in subsequent sections, visit www.jcsocialmarketing.com/socialmediabook.

Visuals and video do not have to be manipulative or pull heartstrings in order to grab attention. They can highlight the mission in action, an impactful moment, even a quiet, intimate conversation or gathering. For example, (RED) showcases beautiful, colorful photos of their field work in the global south, capturing the unique cultures and landscapes in evocative action shots.

Being controversial and a little bit cheeky helps to entice people to pay attention. Plan UK wanted to bring attention to the global issue of child brides, and to make people feel indignant and angry about the issue from a social justice lens. Through their provocative "The Ring" campaign, they showcased celebrities and others "giving child marriage the finger" (using the ring finger) as a way to get people to sit up, stop scrolling, and learn more about this issue.

2. Start with a hook.

If your nonprofit's social media post shows up in your support-er's News Feed, if they click on your blog post from Twitter, if your email newsletter makes it past the Promotions tab in Gmail—you better hook 'em from the start. Every time you communicate with a supporter, the content must be designed to draw people in and spark curiosity from the very first word.

To help educate the public on issues of unfairness in the U.S. worker's compensation system, ProPublica and NPR published an in-depth article, featuring stories of two men living in different states and both suffering devastating workplace injuries. The article which was provocatively titled, "How Much Is Your Arm Worth?" employed powerful visuals to grab your attention and keep you reading.

Anti-sex-trafficking organization Amirah Inc. leverages catchy blog headlines and compelling opening paragraphs to hook readers in and get them to read on. One of their most popular blog posts is entitled "That time I almost died in Honduras" and the opening line is "We have to go. Now." (Be sure to check the reference website listed at the end of the chapter to read the rest of this blog!)

3. Use the element of surprise.

Get risky, get surprising, get shocking. In the must-read marketing bible *Made to Stick*, Chip and Dan Heath write about the importance and the value of surprise in marketing: "When our guessing machines fail, surprise grabs our attention so that we can repair them for the future… Unexpected ideas are more likely to stick because surprise makes us pay attention and think."

Change up the formulaic, predictable structure of your stories and your posts. We need to challenge assumptions, break expectations, and surprise people to keep their attention and to avoid social media fatigue.

In our social media storytelling, we need to use unexpected plot twists, plot structures, and unusual characters. We have to be creative and look beyond the obvious story and the overused case/example mode. Pacing, including suspense and plot twists, plays a huge part in captivating readers or viewers from start to finish.

One of my favorite examples of using surprise to capture attention was during the March For Our Lives in March 2018. Stoneman Douglas High School senior, school shooting survivor, and activist Emma González went inexplicably silent for four minutes and 26 seconds during the March For Our Lives. By shocking the nation with her unexplained minutes of silence, she exemplified what it means to surprise people and grab attention. González went so far off script that the event organizers and her friends came up to her on stage to see if she needed help. By not telling anyone her grand plan, she took a huge risk, made herself vulnerable, and created her own legacy with her bravery and resilience. I will never forget how González stared silently but confidently looked out into the crowd, into the cameras, tears streaming down her face, for what seemed like an eternity. By surprising us all, she grabbed international headlines, and more importantly, her point was made.

One nonprofit that knows how to create buzz by using the element of surprise for social media marketing is PETA. In front of Canada's Parliament, and filmed live on social media, a dozen women, wearing only underwear, drenched themselves in fake blood to protest Canada's commercial seal slaughter.

4. Use subconscious signals.

Music and sounds in video content immediately grab attention and tell us what kind of emotion to feel—scared, happy, joyous, sad, melancholy, etc. When including music or sound in your video, ask what you want people to feel and to think. Music sends a signal to our brain and instructs us on how we should feel (think about the creepy music in a scary movie, or the upbeat music in a romantic comedy). What emotion do you want to convey? Which music best matches that emotion? Top 40 pop? Melancholy string music?

We've all seen it—the infamous ASPCA commercial featuring Sarah McLachlan's song "Angel," and the singer herself sitting on a couch petting a dog. The music in the background, combined with a slideshow of heartbreaking images of abused dogs and cats scrolling across the screen, has raised over $30 million for the animal charity. The heartstring-pulling song put this fundraising campaign on the map.

You don't have to pull heartstrings to grab attention however. The music that you use should always reflect the tone of the video and what you hope to inspire in viewers. In one video, the nonprofit First Descents took a serious, sad topic—"A young adult is diagnosed with cancer every 8 minutes" and made it uplifting and empowering with vibrant imagery and music. Their mission centers around providing free adult adventures for young adults 19-39 years old fighting and surviving cancer, and their message reflects their upbeat and forward-thinking point-of-view.

5. Experiment with innovative technology.

Another way that marketers are grabbing attention is through incorporating new technologies and immersive storytelling into their social media campaigns. By using augmented reality, virtual reality, and 360-degree experiences, savvy nonprofits are bringing supporters into the field and immersing them in the work. This sense of being there and truly seeing the realities on the ground, rather than reading a newspaper article or simply seeing a tweet, engages supporters and creates intense excitement and passion for the cause.

Water Aid gave 360-degree cameras to their staff in the field across the world to shoot interactive, attention-grabbing video of life with the populations they work with and the places they serve. Pencils of Promise created a compelling virtual reality film that transports viewers to a PoP classroom in rural Ghana, showing the transformational effect education can have on a community. Best Friends Animal Society created a virtual reality experience so that people can visit their animal sanctuary in Southern Utah (a 4-hour drive from Las Vegas, the closest airport) without leaving their living rooms.

The only way to grab attention and keep it is by doing the unexpected, the unusual, the creative. For a list of free and low-cost social video tools that you can use to create, enhance, and edit videos, using just your smartphone, visit www.jcsocialmarketing. com/socialmediabook.

Nonprofit Social Media Blueprint: Write down one method you are going to use to grab your audience's attention on social media.

CHAPTER 10

Pillar Two— Content that Elicits Emotion

I've always felt that despite their limited resources, nonprofits have a distinct advantage when they use social media—because of our work, we have an easier time making people angry, or sad, or happy, or inspired. When was the last time your local insurance agent could make you feel extreme passion? (Nothing against insurance agents—they do important work!)

Think about the emotion you felt when you first watched iconic nonprofit videos like Follow the Frog, Caine's Arcade, Kony 2012. The most effective nonprofit marketers take notes on what is currently being shared online and how it makes them feel.

To get engagement, your social media content should have some purpose, some reason to exist. It should spur people to action—it should make people so mad, or so moved, that they can't help but press the share button and tell everyone they know.

There are some common barriers to eliciting an emotion in our social media work. We care deeply, and we want the world to care just as much as we do. We don't understand why they don't! So we give them more and more information, thinking that the more data, information, and statistics we throw at people, the better. The problem is that humans are not rational beings. Our analytical side isn't usually in charge. Often, giving someone *more* information is detrimental to getting them to take action.

Certain experts claim that "90 percent of all purchasing decisions are not made consciously"—the brands that play on our emotions always win our attention and our money. For nonprofits, it can be argued that emotion is even more important to getting people from passive to active.

You absolutely need to elicit some kind of emotion in all of your communications with donors, supporters, and constituents. Your supporters are passionate, motivated, resilient, and most importantly, interested in your cause and your issue! They look to you to inspire them, to create change, and to make a difference.

5 Ways to Elicit Emotion with Your Social Media Content

1. Paint a picture of what's possible.

Too often nonprofits speak in insider terms about the issues we care about—poverty, social justice, climate change, equity. In order to make our ideas accessible to more people, we need to stop using abstract language and instead paint a picture in the mind of our audience of what the concept looks like. Evoke emotion with visual language—this will hold attention and stick in people's memories.

128

Painting a vivid picture in our minds will help sell the vision of the world that you want to create.

Widely regarded as the best orator of the modern age, Martin Luther King, Jr. painted a vivid picture of the future he sought, the future that he wanted people to fight for. One great example of visual language to express an abstract concept is the MLK 'I have a dream' speech: "Let us not seek to satisfy our thirst for freedom by drinking from the cup of bitterness and hatred. We will not be satisfied until justice rolls down like waters, and righteousness like a mighty stream."

U.S. Representative Alexandria Ocasio-Cortez combined narrative, animation, artwork, and vivid imagery in a breakthrough video about the Green New Deal. In the seven minute message sent from 10 years in the future, she describes her vision of the future, a hopeful trajectory for America. The video tells the fictional story of one young girl who's life was transformed because of the Green New Deal, and other policies that Ocasio-Cortez and her fellow representatives implemented.

2. Go beyond manipulation and simple pulling of the heartstrings.

To keep people interested and invested in the work that we do and the problems that we aim to solve, we need to stop relying on simply making people feel sad or guilty. Behavioral science research has shown that people tend to avoid or remain unmoved by messages that:

- Attempt to make them feel bad;
- Obligate them to do something they don't want to do;
- Threaten their identity, values, and worldview.

This is why making people act on complex, wide-ranging issues like poverty, climate change, homelessness, or refugee resettlement is so hard. So much of the current messaging makes people feel guilty and overwhelmed, and they don't know where to start. They feel hopeless.

While "pulling heartstrings" may be initially effective to get people to pay attention, it often becomes numbing, exhausting, and can veer into potentially unethical territory. Instead, we can emphasize growth over hardship. We can tell stories of hope, growth and progress that connect with equal power. People are attracted to things associated with pleasant emotions.

The alternative to evoking guilt in your audience is to share content that is aspirational—make people excited about what's possible! Make people feel hopeful! Pride in community and identity is also a powerful emotion to evoke.

Greenpeace changed their efforts and they now focus on hope rather than fear, anger, or guilt. In their Story & Content Guide, they write:

"The story Greenpeace tells, and has always told, is that a better world is possible, and brave individual and collective actions can make it a reality. Now, to save the world, we're going to get a billion other people to smash their own impossibles. We will tell stories using language that is optimistic, bold and includes a humorous wink. We will rebel against convention and make beauty in the face of dreary and stale."

Mercy Ships uses their social media platforms to share before and after stories of the life-changing surgeries they perform in the developing world countries where they set up shop. Rather than focus on the medical issues and critical deformities they fix, they share stories of hope after the operation. They provide us with a vision of the future they seek to create, where everyone has access to healthcare and medicine.

3. Make it relatable.

To make your social media content relatable, frame stories around the universal human qualities that we all share. For example, many people care about and prioritize family, security, independence, safety, home, and food. Showcase an individual story of hardship overcome in a way that highlights our common humanity and increases empathy. Share artwork, quotes, and other creations from the people that you serve.

UNICEF works in some of the poorest and most remote parts of the world. In their social media content, they don't exploit their subjects by sharing horror stories of war and disease. They take a different tack, sharing relatable, universal stories of families who want safety, education, independence, and healthcare for their children. In one Facebook post, the caption reads:

"A UNICEF South Sudan education worker happened upon these two boys when he was inspecting our looted and burned education supplies in Malakal.

"We miss school," they said.

All children have the right to an education—even in emergencies. #SouthSudanNOW"

The Greater Boston Food Bank uses relatable individual stories of people and families who fell on hard times but are getting back on their feet. One story features Dan, a chef in Gloucester, MA, who had to quit his job when cancer treatments made it impossible to work. He and his family found themselves struggling as medical bills piled up, and sought out help at the local food pantry. This story is relatable on many levels, with heartbreaking tales of struggling to stay afloat due to rising healthcare costs, to being unsure where their next meal would come from.

4. Don't lead with data.

Remember: People fail to act NOT because they do not have enough information, data, and research at their fingertips. Often, they have too much. People fail to act because you haven't made them feel something strongly enough, or they don't understand how their actions can solve a problem. The brain is simply not very good at grasping the implications of mass suffering on a global scale. This is why we are more likely to support one child in need rather than a large group of unnamed children.

Take one of No Kid Hungry's visual storytelling campaigns. It is true that in Arkansas, over 515,000 people struggle with hunger every year—and of them, 32% are children. That statistic may be shocking but it won't necessarily move the needle on your emotions. Instead, the campaign created a message focused on one child: "Save summer for Heather and kids like her." Showing the drastic impact of hunger in the summer for just one child, when schools are closed and free meals aren't readily available, is much more powerful and memorable.

The New York Times knew that the Syrian refugee crisis, with millions of displaced people all over the world, was too large and complex a topic for most Americans to wrap their brains around. To make it more relatable and to better shed light on what the refugees experience, they followed one Syrian family and documented their journey to America and their resettlement over a six-month period in 2016. The outpouring of support, empathy, and money was overwhelming, because people saw their own family reflected in the struggle to find safety and security across borders.

5. Show more than you tell.

Rather than telling the reader or the viewer exactly what is happening in the photo, the video, or the post, show them through compelling imagery. Don't over explain, use insider speak, or jargon—remember that people unfamiliar with an issue will have a hard time processing all the intricacies and complexities of it. Show the impact of the work through video or photography, or in a compelling quote from a client.

On Instagram, to raise awareness and money in the wake of Hurricane Maria, Feeding America posted visual stories directly from the frontlines. These raw photos of homes and communities destroyed showed supporters exactly what was happening on the ground, beyond the news headlines and mainstream media coverage.

In their communications via email and on social media, the Kibera School for Girls in Ghana lets the students tell their own stories in their own words. They even take their own photos to share. The girls who attend the school share poems, artwork, and assignments they completed due to the generosity of donors funding their education.

Activity: On the Social Media Blueprint, write down one way that you can elicit an emotion from your audience on social media.

CHAPTER 11

Pillar Three–
Content that Demonstrates Impact

Social media provides you with an opportunity to showcase your distinctive and unique footprint on the world. Your impact is not the "what" of the services you provide—it's the WHY. Focus on the benefits you provide, not the nuts and bolts features of the programs. Even if your organization doesn't directly serve individuals or animals, you should be able to show some tangible impact of your work in terms that lay people can understand—otherwise, it's going to be difficult to recruit people into your cause.

To best create content that demonstrates impact, answer the following questions:

- What generally draws supporters to your work?
- Why are they passionate about this issue?
- What do you do best?

- What is special about your organization?
- In what unique ways are you making the world a better place?
- What problem are you solving, and why do you have the solution?

5 Ways to Demonstrate Impact with Your Social Media Content

1. Tell evocative stories.

The absolute best way to reach hearts and minds and to convince people of your impact is through sharing stories of transformation and change. To provide the most agency to the people you serve and to avoid exploitation, these stories are best told by individuals or small groups in their own words, with little to no editing.

Sharing the stories of those that benefit from your work is a perfect way to show stakeholders the direct result of their support. Storytelling makes complex issues more tangible to audiences that aren't inside the work every single day.

Filmed in Nepal, Chuna shares her experiences of being a girl in a traditional culture that would not let her get an education. But she still wanted to learn, and the READ center helped her accomplish this lifelong dream. Her story is one of ambition and transformation, as she now wants to help other illiterate women in her community learn to read.

"I got my daughter back," says Mia's mother. Mia came to Rise Academy in the fifth grade significantly behind, but rediscovered her confidence and skipped four grade levels in reading in one year. The story of Mia and her mother, and how Rise Academy helped get Mia back on track in school and in her family relationships, is a perfect example of evocative storytelling to showcase transformation and impact. What parent or caregiver wouldn't tear up listening to this very relatable story?

2. Use data visualization.

Showcasing impact can come in many forms, not just in emotional videos or photos of the people that you serve. Nonprofits can create a visually interesting annual impact report and share them across social media platforms, in an email, and on their websites.

Girls Who Code creates and shares multimedia annual reports on their website. Explore working with a graphic designer or using DIY graphic design tools to create a visual depiction of your annual report that can be shared easily on social media. Infographics are also popular on social media and a great way to highlight data and make it visually interesting.

3. Gather content from your supporters.

Your online community has a wealth of information and stories at their fingertips. Your job is to encourage and incentivize them to share publicly to their networks! Simply asking people to "Share your story!" on social media won't work—it's too vague and too overwhelming for busy people who may want to participate but don't want to tell their entire story online. Encourage them to participate by showcasing the stories of others like them who have shared photos, videos, and information. Model best practices and show your audience what you would like them to contribute.

A great example of content generated from your supporters (also called UGC—user-generated content) is the fabulous and powerful #UniteForParkinsons campaign. Each year on April 11 the world commemorates World Parkinson's Day to raise awareness of the condition and change attitudes. The purpose of the campaign was to show what living with Parkinson's is truly like, so Parkinson's UK asked people with Parkinson's all over the world to submit videos ahead of the day. The two simple instructions that they sent to their followers were to be honest, brave and real and to show that Parkinson's is much more than just a tremor. People posted video to give an authentic and powerful insight into their lives.

Best Buddies builds one-to-one friendships between people of similar ages with and without intellectual and developmental disabilities (IDD). On their social media channels, Best Buddies reshares (with permission) stories, quotes, and intimate moments of the participants in their Friendship Programs, clearly showcasing the impact that the organization has had on both parties involved.

4. Highlight the significance of one project.

For many nonprofits, the issues that they tackle are diverse, complex, and multi-faceted. Organizations often juggle multiple programs and services, each seeking recognition and promotion on social media. The result is a jumble of disjointed social media posts that don't provide an accurate picture of the organization and that confuse and bewilder the audience. To make it simpler for your social media community to understand, try to highlight the work of one project and the impact that it made.

Take the example of CHOICE Humanitarian, a nonprofit focused on ending extreme poverty in rural areas. The average person is not likely to understand the complex ways in which development projects contribute to the larger goal of ending poverty. On their blog and on Facebook, CHOICE shares bite-size pieces of information and short stories about specific projects and individuals to help us understand how the pieces fit together.

Rosie's Place in Boston provides over a dozen programs and services to their guests, including emergency services, ESL classes, legal services, outreach, mental health care, food assistance, and more. In order to inspire action on social media, they often highlight just one story related to a single aspect of their work to make their impact more tangible and easy to grasp.

5. Don't sugarcoat the work.

Yes, you are changing your little corner of the world for good. You are making a difference and transforming lives, the environment, and the community in positive, powerful ways. Society is a better place with you in it. But, as we know all too well, the work is hard, treacherous, full of obstacles and minefields. Not every program succeeds, not every client survives, not every story is tied up in a bow with a happy ending. If you work in the field of homelessness, or poverty eradication, or social justice, it's not reasonable or responsible to only show your supporters the success stories. Life doesn't usually work out that way, and the majority of your audience knows this. Don't sugarcoat or gloss over the hard stuff about what you do to get to those small wins and to create change—we want to see the bumps and bruises that you got along the way.

The St. Baldrick's Foundation raises money to fund vital cancer research and supportive care for children and families that have experienced a cancer diagnosis. They share a combination of inspiration and gratitude in their Facebook posts, but they are not afraid to tell their audience about the stark reality of dealing with childhood cancer, and elicit emotions of empathy and sadness to compel people to action.

Plummer Youth Promise, a small foster care nonprofit north of Boston, shares honest and raw stories about what it's like to find "forever families" for older black males in their program. They write about the stark realities of the foster care system, writing often with an emotional hook and inviting the audience to consider the questions that the young adults in their program often tackle: "Who would come to my funeral?" and "Who is going to come to my graduation?"

Activity: On the Social Media Blueprint, write down one way that you can showcase the impact of your work on social media.

CHAPTER 12

Pillar Four– Content that Builds Trust

A main focus of all nonprofit communications work should be to gain the trust of your audience. In order to build a community that will take action on your behalf, and especially to raise money, you must inspire trust in your programs, your services, and your impact.

Nonprofits should aim to become an indispensable go-to resource for their fans and followers. Think about your personal social media behavior: Why do you follow, like, and share certain pages, organizations, brands, and people on social media? Which email newsletters keep your interest and get you reading them week after week? Which blogs do you frequent and subscribe to?

Your audience is looking to you as a trusted, credible expert on the issue that they care about. After all, you are in the trenches, working hard on this problem every single day, trying to find solutions. In order to be considered an expert, not only must you provide valuable insights, but you must also take a firm stance. Think about the types of information (statistics, stories, photos) that your nonprofit has access to that your donors and supporters do not. How can you teach them, educate and inform them on this topic that is close to their hearts?

5 Ways to Build Trust with Your Social Media Content

1. Be the go-to resource in your industry.

Become an authority on your cause. Back up your stories and your social media content with evidence. Maintain your credibility by accurately citing your sources and imagery. Be objective and professional. It's important to note that being this go-to resource is NOT about what you want to tell your audience—it's about what they want to know, learn, and hear about.

Girl power nonprofit A Mighty Girl creates and shares an annual Holiday Gift Guide, which helps parents and others interested in girls empowerment to purchase inspirational gifts. Amirah, Inc. also creates a Holiday Gift Guide, highlighting their favorite products from brands that employ and empower survivors of sex trafficking.

The American Red Cross does a stellar job of sharing helpful, relevant information with it's Facebook fans, and is an invaluable go-to resource during natural disasters. When Hurricane Iscllc/ Julio was approaching Hawaii in 2014, the Red Cross shared a list of items to have on hand, and what to do in case of an emergency.

2. Aim to inform and educate.

Your audience is busy with their everyday lives and responsibilities. They care about the causes that they support, but they aren't able to stay on top of all the news and announcements surrounding the issues. That's where nonprofits come in. We are on the frontlines and we have an insider view of the cause and the problem. Aim to hold regular educational sessions with your audience, via webinar or live video broadcast.

Our Health California holds regular webcasts on issues of importance and relevance to their supporters. A sample post: "Please join our webcast this Thursday, Jan. 17, to learn how leaders in California are working on local initiatives to ramp up clean mobility even faster and to equitably bring electric vehicles into their communities."

Determine what kind of information your online community is searching for and give it to them. The National Aphasia Association got to the first page in Google search by focusing their website and social media content on the types of things their community was searching for—aphasia types, symptoms, and treatments.

3. Show your human side.

Can people see the humanity in your content? Do they know that there are people behind the posts and tweets? People crave access, authenticity, and transparency from the causes they support. Show that there are humans behind your social media accounts.

NPR editor Christopher Dean Hopkins accidentally posted about his not yet one-year-old daughter Ramona on NPR's official Facebook page. Horrified, Hopkins deleted the post and wrote an apology. The problem was that everyone wanted Ramona back! Hashtags like #ramonaupdates, #bringbackramona, #ramonaforever took over the internet, and even the Houston Zoo got involved, asking about Ramona and her cat obsession.

Instagram Stories are a great way to experiment with raw, authentic content. Susan G. Komen Florida share Stories from the field, scouting locations for their next race or walk, talking with volunteers, buying donuts, and showing staff members having a great time doing the work.

4. Share social proof.

No organization can successfully exist in a silo without great volunteers, Board members, sponsors, donors, and community partners. Share information about the people in the community that help make your work possible, and that believe in you and support you.

Social proof can also take the form of a write-up in the local paper or a prestigious award that acknowledges your hard work and impact.

The Greater Boston Food Bank's CEO is often a featured expert in news stories about unemployment and food insecurity in the region. They then share these articles to social media, tying it to their mission, with a call to action to learn more about their services.

If you have a local celebrity or other influential person who is prepared to support you publicly, share their story. Local nonprofit Girls Inc. of Lynn and jewelry designer Hearts on Fire joined local news broadcaster and celebrity Latoyia Edwards in a Facebook Live discussion about their new partnership to design and develop a new collection of jewelry.

5. Be accessible and transparent.

When you open the social media can of worms, it's inevitable that people will try to contact you and message you via those sites. In order to be accessible, encourage this two-way communication by answering questions and comments promptly and honestly. Be transparent about trials and challenges faced at your organization (where public and where appropriate, of course). If you decide to change course on a program that isn't working, or if you decide not to take grant money or work with a certain corporate sponsor, share the reasons and the process with your online community. Show that you are a good steward of funds and of trust, and that you walk the walk for your clients and your cause.

Committed to transparency and accessibility in philanthropy, Bill & Melinda Gates Foundation CEO Sue Desmond-Hellmann often takes questions and comments from viewers live on Facebook. Viewers can ask questions about currently funded projects, planned activities, and trends in the sector as well as express their opinions on the topic at hand.

Activity: On the Social Media Blueprint, write down one way that you can build and inspire trust with your social media content.

CHAPTER 13

Pillar Five– Content that Inspires Conversation

Facebook has told us that the posts that work best on the platform are those that "inspire conversation" and elicit "meaningful interactions." To capitalize on this knowledge, ask: What information can you offer and share that no other group can? Is there a hot topic that you know your audience wants to hear your opinion on? Give it to them with your solid stance and then ask them if they agree and why/why not. Encourage healthy debate and discussion on your social media channels. Always remember that social media was built for conversations, not as a billboard to push out messages.

5 Ways to Inspire Conversation with Your Social Media Content

1. Get provocative.

One surefire way to spark conversation is provocation. This approach may seem risky to nonprofits, who tend to want to avoid conflict and negative comments at all costs. However, provoking a reaction by doing the unexpected can pay off in engagement.

UNICEF UK does this in a unique way by turning the rules of social media platform Pinterest on its head. On the surface, Pinterest seems pretty shallow to some people. It is often referred to as an extension of rampant consumerism, just another online shopping list; a voyeuristic view into the needless items we covet and desire. To flip the script, UNICEF is posting compelling images of things that people in the world really want and need— to survive. They created a fictional profile for a 13-year-old girl named Ami Musa, from the poor, war-torn African country of Sierra Leone. Ami's one and only board is called "Really want these" and instead of Louboutins, iPhone cases, and nail art she's dying to try, Ami's pinned images include plain rice, faucets for clean drinking water, and chalk for school. If you click on the photos on Ami's pin board, you are taken to a simple donation landing page at the UNICEF website with a photo of "Ami" and the text: "Children like Ami need basics that many of us take for granted: food, education, healthcare, a clean supply of water. Your donation can help us provide these and other essentials. Thank you." The effect is jarring and caused a lot of online discussion.

The Be Real Campaign was formed to create a movement and conversation around body positivity and body confidence. By sharing heartfelt stories and photographs of real people and their unretouched bodies, they are changing the regular Instagram feed that tends towards highly-filtered and photoshopped celebrities in perfect posts. The campaign encourages others to participate, give feedback, and ask questions.

2. Be timely and relevant.

We know that social media algorithms reward content that is timely, trending, and relevant. Your nonprofit can inspire conversation by commenting on news and trending topics as they happen. This is especially vital if you want to mobilize support around a specific issue as it unfolds in the public eye.

Choose a story in the news and add your contribution in one or two paragraphs. Discuss why this is important and how it relates back to the issue and the cause you are working on. Why is it important, why did you choose it, what does it add to the overall discussion? If you are skittish about taking a stand or expressing an opinion, simply cite the facts and ask your online community what they think and what they would do.

When Bob Kraft, owner of the New England Patriots, was arrested for alleged solicitation of prostitutes, anti-sex trafficking nonprofit Amirah Inc. knew that people would have a lot of questions and opinions—especially in their home region. They took to social media to provide their unique expertise and perspective on this issue, having worked to #savesurvivors and raise awareness about the issue of sex slavery in New England since 2009.

REACH Beyond Domestic Violence shares op-eds, articles, and blog posts that relate to their core principles and that are useful to their community, while adding their expert perspective on current events related to sexual violence and abuse.

3. Ask questions.

One of the best ways to inspire genuine conversation inside your social media communities is to ask questions. Questions should not be vague or overly open-ended, rather they should be focused and easy to answer in one-two sentences.

Edutopia poses fun trivia and other discussion questions on it's Instagram account to entertain its audience and get them participating. These include: "What the best April Fool's Prank you ever played?" to "What would you like to see schools investing in?"

The Caregiver Action Network often asks for caregiving tips and advice from it's online community, that it then shares on the networks' social media accounts.

4. Go live.

Leverage live streaming for interaction and participation in real time. Live streaming video is consistently the most engaging type of content on social media—Facebook claims that live videos are watched three times longer than recorded videos, and get 10 times as many comments and engagements. Use live streaming for in-the-moment comments and feedback from viewers and supporters.

Best Friends Animal Society frequently goes live on their Facebook page to showcase their staff in the field, explain the nitty gritty details of their work, show off their beautiful sanctuary in Southern Utah, and interact with their community members in real time.

The Metropolitan Museum of Art enlisted Brinda Kumar, a researcher and curator of the "Nasreen Mohamedi" exhibition, to walk viewers in real time through the exhibition with Sree Sreenivasan, The Met's Chief Digital Officer. This real-time interaction with people who work at the Met serves to break down walls and encourages people to ask questions, driving engagement and raising awareness of its latest exhibition.

5. Thank your online community members.

People love to be acknowledged and thanked for their contributions, and it's a staple of any successful donor relations program. Using social media, you can thank your supporters in real time and encourage them to tell you why they showed up and why they took action.

On Giving Tuesday 2018, the No Kid Hungry campaign live streamed a "Wall of Thanks" on Periscope via Twitter to give shout-outs to donors, supporters, volunteers, and community members in real time.

The Wellbody Alliance takes to its blog and social media channels twice per week in November to express gratitude for their donors, employees, volunteers, and partners. Through visuals and graphics, Wellbody tells the story of one or more people they feature.

Activity: On the Social Media Blueprint, write down one way that you can inspire conversation amongst your audience members using social media.

CHAPTER 14

Pillar Six–
Content that Encourages Sharing

Social psychologist Dr. Sander van der Linden says the key to creating a viral social movement is the creation of a shared identity between the individual and the cause over time. How can your social media content help to create this shared identity? Can you focus on optimism, inspiration, and aspiration? When you share something on social media, your community should say, both to themselves and in public, "This reflects me and my values, what I believe, what I stand for! I'm so proud to be a part of this!"

This is, in effect, what the most effective and timeless brands do. They create a community, not just a group of customers. Theodore McManus, the advertising genius who built Cadillac, Dodge, and Chrysler to name a few, thought of a brand as something to be trusted and revered. He didn't work with companies that just wanted a quick and easy sale, but ones that wanted long-term loyalty. He created car brands where the car was transformed from a simple status symbol to an actual part of someone's identity.

Content that builds this kind of passionate community encourages others to spread the message. Social media is a perfect representation of a service that incentivizes people to bring in their friends, their family, and their professional networks. If you are the only person that you know on Facebook, the platform is not any good to you. But if *everyone you know is using it*, the experience gets exponentially better. The incentive then becomes to bring more and more people into the fold. The same should be said for your nonprofit's online community.

We all know that sharing is the gold standard of social media. Likes and comments are all well and good, but getting someone to share, to retweet, to repin, to regram—that is what ultimately exposes your content to a wider audience. Sharing is more powerful as it requires more engagement than passively scrolling, reading or even clicking "like" on a post.

When a member of your online community shares your content with their network, this gets new eyeballs on your information and hopefully brings more of the right people into the fold. So how do we get more members of our online communities to share our content? We spread the word when it benefits us, our status, our standing. We share content that makes us *feel* good and *look* good to our networks.

5 Ways to Encourage Sharing with Your Social Media Content

1. Preach to the choir.

I am a firm believer in nonprofits preaching to the choir. We spend too much time focused on "standing out" and "cutting through the clutter," just to get our message in front of the wrong audiences—people that will never care about and/or agree with what we stand for.

Preach to the choir, and encourage them to share your message with other like-minded individuals. You have people in your circle who already know your work, believe in you, and like you. It's 10x more effective to convince people to take action if they know something about you. It's much more expensive, time-consuming, and difficult to convince non-believers to come on board.

Planned Parenthood Action Network creates shareable social media graphics designed with sharing in mind, knowing that their community will be inspired to post them on their accounts.

The Human Rights Campaign (HRC) is another example of how a nonprofit can effectively preach to the choir by truly understanding what will resonate with their specific audience, even while alienating others. They create social media graphics focused on their audience and their community.

2. Let the community participate in building it.

If your online community is an active participant in designing and building the content or the platform, they will be more invested in sharing it and promoting it to others.

The Washington Trails Association created the community-led review site Hike Finder Map (think Yelp for hikers). They wanted to provide a needed service and fill a gap for their target audience, as well as invest in technology that would help them fulfill their mission. The Hike Finder Map encourages participants to leave reviews and empowers them to protect these wild places. Hikers found this interactive map incredibly useful, but only if they could get a critical mass of people using it. The incentive to share it far and wide was born.

The Montana Wilderness Association wanted to reach more members of hard-to-reach audiences, like young professionals and parents of young children. The organization created Wilderness Walks, a free, open-to-the-public program that showcases the "why" of their mission (protecting wildness) and recruits advocates to spread the word on social media to other like-minded people. The more people who take part, the better the service, the increased reach on social media, and the more Walks they can provide.

3. Host a social media takeover.

A great way to get increased visibility for your social media content is to hand the keys over to a trusted supporter (or two or three). Social media takeovers, where a member of your online community manages a specific social media account for the day or the week, are becoming low-cost ways for nonprofits to build their audiences and share fresh content.

Instagram takeovers are a hot new trend, especially among higher ed institutions and those who serve younger populations. UK mental health charity Mind has truly embraced the power and the fun nature of Instagram Stories by allowing their supporters to occasionally take over the account and post their own content as they undertake a fundraising challenge.

4. Learn what's most shareable on social and copy it.

Conduct research on the latest trends in social media and adapt them for your nonprofit. Popular content types like memes and GIFs are imminently shareable, because they are entertaining, humorous, and make people smile.

Inspirational quotes from famous authors, politicians, and celebrities are shared widely on social media. You can look to the web to find them, or create your own using low-cost design tools like the WordSwag mobile app or Canva.com/nonprofits.

Memes are taking the internet by storm. A meme shows an image, video or text that has been altered—often in a humorous or creative way—and spread rapidly by internet users. You can use free sites like Meme Generator, Imgflip, or Make A Meme to create and adapt your own.

5. Give your audience quick wins.

Behavioural science teaches us that small actions taken on behalf of an organization or brand make us more likely to say yes to the next ask. Provide your audience with small, quick wins that will help them immediately see the results of participation on your social media platforms, and you will start to build a deeper relationship with them. Use the example of the wildly popular smartphone game Angry Birds—the company intentionally makes the first level so easy so that players get a quick win, and become hooked.

Your nonprofit may be running low on dish soap or paper towels and you have a large program tonight or a big support group meeting—let people know on social media. People love the instant gratification of satisfying an immediate need, and if they are already at the grocery store and see your tweet or Facebook post, they may be inclined to purchase items in the moment.

Naperville Area Humane Society in Illinois was running out of kitty litter one day at their no-kill animal shelter, so they tweeted about it. The community responded in an overwhelming way.

To this day, they still receive bags of kitty litter, which they can stockpile or give away to families who adopt the cats they house.

Other examples of social media quick wins:

- Homeless shelters can post on Facebook that they need travel items to make Welcome packages for people in the shelter.
- Food banks can tweet about immediate needs of perishable items.
- After-school programs can ask for school supplies, office supplies, arts and crafts supplies.
- Child care centers can tweet to ask for donations of gently-used toys or other necessary items.

Activity: On the Social Media Blueprint, write down one way that you can encourage your audience to share your content on social media.

CHAPTER 15

How to Repurpose Existing Content

Unless your nonprofit just formed yesterday, you most likely have at least a few photos, videos, appeal letters, annual reports, grant proposals, and the like cluttering up your hard drive and your filing cabinets. You may also have posted and shared on social media for a few months or years, sent out email newsletters, and published a blog. All of this took hard work, time, creativity, and resources to put out in the world. So why not take another look at it and see if it can be utilized again in other ways?

Don't reinvent the wheel! There are many ways to repurpose and recycle the great content that you already have, with a few tweaks and a fresh coat of paint.

The first step is to conduct a quick Communications Audit. Conducting an audit and inventory of your past and current nonprofit communications is not as daunting and complicated as it seems. To start, I recommend looking broadly at your social media efforts from the last three months. (If you are starting 100% from scratch and don't have any presence on social media, take a look at any external communications work that you have done: emails, annual reports, letters, press releases, etc.)

Look at the platforms where you have been consistently active for the last three months. If you have not posted on a particular platform in over three months, we will consider that platform DOA for the moment. If you have a social media measurement tool like HubSpot or HootSuite that can run a report for you, use it. If you don't, you will need to go manually through the insights or analytics section for each platform.

Look over your posts, tweets, articles, videos, photos, and other types of content that you have shared over the past three months. When we get into the measurement part of this section, that's where we will determine exact metrics of success and build out a spreadsheet to track them.

For our initial, quick and dirty social media audit here, I only want you to write down four things.

- Two posts that you noticed worked better than most, that you think could be replicated or adapted and used again.

- Two posts that didn't work as well as you had hoped, but that you think could be improved.

Do you notice any trends? What can you extrapolate from what worked and what didn't work so well? What kinds of content—videos, live streams, photos, stories—worked best? What topics worked best? What types of content fell flat? What learnings and insight can you glean from this? Write down everything that comes to mind, and keep it close, as it will help plan out content for your Social Media Calendar.

As an example, one press release or annual appeal letter can be adapted into an unlimited number of other content pieces, including:

- Slide deck with bullet points
- Blog post
- Pinterest infographic
- LinkedIn article
- Facebook update
- Video summary

Here are 10 more ways that you can repurpose existing communication and fundraising materials into social media gold:

1. Made-For-You Video

Take your long blog posts, press releases, or research reports and convert them into video. Video editing software Lumen5 will transform your text document or bulleted list into a video perfect for social media. Using their pre-designed Smart Templates, you can upload an original blog post or text document and it will create a customized video for you, or you can create a completely original slideshow video manually. All videos use Lumen5 stock images (for free) and their own stock music (for free). You can then share the video to social media or download the file and embed into a blog. To see a free video that Lumen5 created based on a blog post that I wrote, visit www.jcsocialmarketing.com/socialmediabook

There are a variety of mobile apps and desktop tools, like Magisto and Animoto, that take your existing photos and video clips and edit them together into a beautiful video montage, complete with music and subtitles.

2. Video Clips

Take snippets of a longer video, such as a livestream broadcast or YouTube video, and chop it up into shorter snackable video clips perfect for social media. Apps like Storeo and CutStory will take a large video file and cut it down to shorter videos of custom length.

3. Slide Decks

PDFs and presentation slides can be uploaded into the website SlideShare, with a customized description and title, then shared as a link across social networks. You can feature SlideShare posts on your LinkedIn profile, or embed the slide decks directly inside blog posts or other pages on your website.

4. Pull-quote Graphics

Use a free graphic design tool like Canva or Adobe Spark to create pull-quotes or visual highlights from longer form content. Canva has hundreds of thousands of templates, automatic resizing, and a stock photo library chock full of free options; it's the go-to place for non-graphic designers who don't like PhotoShop. You can pull out highlights from a longer blog post, news interview, bulleted list, or presentation and create perfect square or vertical graphics for social media.

5. Infographics

Infographics make data and text easier to consume, digest, and remember. Create an infographic from your annual report. There are many infographic tools on the market that make your life even easier because of the import feature—import data directly from spreadsheets rather than entering it all manually. For storytelling purposes, you want to walk people through the story visually.

6. Instagram and Facebook Stories

Instagram and Facebook Stories are exploding in popularity, and if your nonprofit has a presence on Instagram, it's time to start experimenting. Adobe Spark Post offers a simple, easy way to create beautiful graphics to upload to your Instagram Story, to make it look more professional and well-designed. Chunk your information into pieces, using pull-quotes, statistics, and "do you know" data, and create graphics to add to your Instagram Story. DoSomething. org posts well-designed Instagram and Facebook Stories on their accounts.

7. E-books

Creating short e-books in PowerPoint is easier than ever, or you can use free customizable ebook templates from Canva, Visme, and Lucidpress. Turn your stories, annual reports, case studies, grant proposals, and more into beautiful PDF e-books to share on your website or via social media channels. Add great photos and you have a visual storytelling asset that can be updated and used for years to come.

8. Guest Posting

If you have a great story or news announcement to share about your work, write a blog post and explore other sites that may be interested in publishing it. Many of the nonprofit news websites like *The Chronicle of Philanthropy* and *NonProfit PRO* accept guest contributors. Also explore nonprofit software companies that have a regularly updated blog, like Bloomerang, NeonCRM, Classy, CauseVox, NTEN, and Wild Apricot. Do some research by reading several blog posts on the site to which you want to contribute, to get a feel of what they like to publish. Then approach their editor with your idea, or even your fully finished post.

9. Live Event

Google Hangout is completely free, available to all, and super easy to set up and use. Facebook and Instagram Live are also free. If you are sending out an email or a press release announcing an event or new program, consider sharing this via live video. Make sure you promote the time and date to your fans, followers, and email list. Once the live broadcast has ended, you can embed the video file on your blog or on your website, and share the link out via other social media channels.

10. Blog (not what you think)

So many nonprofits feel that blogs have to be expertly-written, longform, and planned weeks in advance. But that's wrong! The Blog section of your website can be used to embed and re-purpose your most popular social media posts, your live stream videos, photos with short captions, event updates, and more. You do not have to have a professional copywriter on your team to leverage that section of your website. Use it to document what you do and re-share social media posts or news articles, adding your unique perspective and commentary.

Activity: On the Social Media Blueprint, choose three items from your content archives, online or offline, that you can repurpose, and then write down ideas in the second column.

Piece of Content	Ways to Repurpose
(Example) Facebook Live video taken at the gala	1. Embed into blog post 2. Cut into short clips and share on Stories 3. Create a pull-quote graphic

CHAPTER 16

How to Curate Content From Outside Sources

The most effective and efficient nonprofit social media managers know that hand-crafting every piece of social media content from scratch is not practical, nor is it realistic. We need to become content curators and have our eyes and ears open for outside content that could be relevant and interesting to our audience.

Content curation is the act of collecting, filtering, and sharing the best information on a specific topic for a specific audience. Compare social media content curation to the work of a museum curator. Museum art curators choose a theme for an exhibit, they select the best paintings to fit that theme, they annotate the paintings, and display them in a way that makes sense to the consumer.

A good content curator continually seeks, makes sense of, and shares the best and most relevant content on a particular topic. They add their own thoughts and spin to the post, explaining why they selected to share it with the community. It's not as much about spraying out links to articles as you come across them—it's about finding relevant materials amid the noise and clutter online, organizing it, and adding your perspective so it adds even more value to your audience.

Here are five main content curation strategies to further educate and engage your community by keeping the social media machine fresh and relevant.

Employ social listening strategies to keep tabs on your audience's interests.

Social listening is not simply monitoring notifications and mentions of your organization across the social web. Effective social listening analyzes the conversations and trends happening not just around your specific organization, but around your industry, cause, and issue and then using those insights to make better marketing decisions.

Listening brings you into the larger conversation and context around your issue. It allows you to gain a deeper insight into your audience, what they talk about, what they care about, and how they talk about these issues. Having a social listening strategy for your marketing will show you the vocabulary, terminology, and language that your audience uses so that you can then craft your communications appropriately. Some digital dashboards for social listening include HootSuite, Buffer, Meltwater, Mention.com, and Attentive. ly (get the full list at www.jcsocialmarketing.com/socialmediabook)

Keep a list of topics your audience will be interested in.

To avoid overwhelm, hone in and be laser-focused on your online community's characteristics, needs, and preferences. Refer back to your Nonprofit Social Media Blueprint, identifying what your audience wants. When evaluating whether or not to share an article or video from an outside source, ask the following questions:

- Is this adding to my audience's knowledge of, and education on the issue?
- Is this a topic of relevance and interest?
- What are they getting out of this?
- What do they want to get out of this?
- What do they hope to learn?
- How do they want to feel?

Comment on current events and news.

Share relevant news stories or create your own to keep your community informed about the issue you care about. Sign up for Google Alerts, free emails that you receive daily or weekly featuring the latest news on a topic of your choosing. Sign up to get a Google Alert for your cause, for example, "domestic violence," "wetlands preservation," or "animal abuse". You should also set up a news alert for your organization's name and the city, state, or region that you serve. When you come across an article or a news story that would be of interest to your audience, think about how you can thoughtfully and purposefully add to the discussion. Choose an article or blog post (or video or photo, etc.) and write two paragraphs about the issue and explain clearly why your audience should pay attention. Make sure to cite the original source and link back to the article.

A pro tip is to focus not just on your organization's name and industry, but track competitor brands, collaborators and partners, industry buzzwords, relevant hashtags, and media outlets and reports that cover your issue.

Share visual data on the issue.

Along with creating your own graphics, search Pinterest or Google for your issue plus the word "infographic"—i.e. "transgender rights infographic" or "food insecurity infographic". Find the source of the infographic that you want to use, and contact them to see if you can share it publicly. When you share it, be sure to add your unique thoughts and perspective, summing up the most interesting data points of the infographic. Make sure to cite the original source and link back to the original creator where possible.

Use content curation tools.

Free online tools Scoop.it and List.ly are great places to curate interesting information around a specific topic before sharing it on social networks. Sign up for a free account on either site. Identify up to three topics that are relevant to your mission, your cause, and your audience. With Scoop.it, you can post a link to your desired social media platform and then add your own insight. You can then share it to all your social media sites for further exposure.

Make lists of thought leaders to follow.

Make a list of five-10 thought leaders in your space that you follow. Subscribe to their email newsletters, YouTube channels, their blogs, and follow them on social media. To cut down on the clutter on Twitter, make a list of your top 10 thought leaders using Twitter lists. You can then refer to that list and filter out their tweets in your Twitter feed. The key is to focus on those who provide you AND your audience with valuable content. When you are looking to fill in your editorial calendar, you can turn to this list to find information to share.

Effective content curation takes time and effort to do well. However, it can be a perfect compliment to content creation efforts like writing a blog, sending out a regular email newsletter and posting regularly on social media.

Activity: On the Social Media Blueprint, write down one tool that you can use to research and curate content for your community.

CHAPTER 17

How to Address Five Common Nonprofit Social Media Challenges

For every nonprofit that was an early adopter of social media, there is another one that has not yet embraced this revolution in communications. While every nonprofit faces unique obstacles, in my nonprofit work spanning almost two decades, I have encountered some common themes when it comes to digital marketing and social media.

In the Introduction to this book I laid out the five essential marketing mindset shifts required of modern nonprofit marketers and change agents. Beyond simply shifting mindsets (which is imperative to succeeding in this work), there are certain realities and roadblocks that many nonprofits face when sharing their work on social media.

In this chapter, I will address five of the most prevalent challenges that nonprofits face when enacting a successful social media strategy. Some of these seemingly insurmountable roadblocks often stop nonprofit social media managers before they start. I won't let you get off that easy however—for each challenge, I will provide a tactical solution to get you out of the rut and move you forward.

Confidentiality: We can't share client faces and names.

I ran the development shop (i.e. me, myself and I) at a small nonprofit serving women and children who had experienced domestic and sexual violence, so I understand the issue of confidentiality very well. In many cases, even if they wanted to share their stories or to talk about their experiences, the clients' identities needed to be protected for their physical safety.

If you are committed to creating a community using social media, storytelling and sharing the personal experiences of those you serve is a huge part of it. Sharing impact stories and testimonials on social media is the best way to make your online community feel like they are making a difference and a meaningful contribution.

If you work for an organization that needs to be careful when it comes to client identities and social media, here are some ideas:

- Speak with alumni of the program to gather success stories and photos to share on social media. At the domestic violence program where I worked, the program staff kept in close contact with several of the families who had moved on from the program and were leading successful, healthy lives. Some of your program alumni may be willing to help you.

- Collect stories from your donors as to why they give, and from your volunteers as to why they volunteer. They all have stories of their own and a reason to be giving back to your organization, some of them will welcome the opportunity to share it with others.

- Find a local celebrity or influential personality. At the program where I worked, we contacted a local news anchor who lost a sister to domestic violence to come speak at our annual breakfast. She spoke eloquently and emotionally about how she wished that her sister could have found a program like ours—it may have saved her life.

- Never assume that the people you work with don't want to participate on social media, or share their own stories. I am positive that there are clients, volunteers, staff and others in your community that you have touched who are willing and able to share their perspectives publicly.

- Always be mindful of the people that you serve. Sharing a vulnerable experience publicly is incredibly powerful, but it can also be draining and painful. Make sure that the people you work with and serve feel like they are helping to create real change, and not just providing materials for the next Facebook post. And most importantly, respect people's opinions and their right to privacy, even if they originally say they will help and then change their minds.

- Shield personal details and use a creatively-staged photo. There are tons of free and low-cost stock photography sites available. Warning—use stock photos strategically and thoughtfully! Do not use an image that you have seen a million times or one that is very generic looking and uninspiring.

- Use graphic design and photo editing tools like Canva and WordSwag to crop photos, edit photos, and add text overlay.

We don't have a sexy cause.

You don't provide direct services to children or animals, and thus feel like your impact and your stories won't resonate on social media. Real talk—a LOT of the work we do in the sector is thankless, controversial, and certainly not sexy! I'm a firm believer that there are no "unsexy" causes, just "unconfident" or "uncreative" marketers! Just because you don't have toddlers and puppies running around does not mean that you can't succeed in building up a passionate community on social media.

We know that sexiness is really a state of mind. It's all about confidence and how you put yourself out there. It's about how someone carries themselves, how they behave, and how they present to the world. For nonprofits, this philosophy applies as well.

- If you think your cause is "unsexy"—everyone else will too.
- If you think your stories are not compelling—everyone else will too.
- If you think your work is boring—everyone else will too.
- If you aren't excited about your cause—why would anyone else get excited?

You need to instill more confidence in the value of your work and the potential power of your messages. The reality is that there are thousands, hundreds of thousands, of nonprofits and worthy social causes competing for attention on social media. But if you aren't clear on the unique value that you provide to the world, as well as who cares about your cause, it won't matter if you spend $5,000 on Facebook Ads, or use Instagram Stories. The medium is not as important as the message.

How to get more confidence in your mission and lose the "unsexy" complex:

- Stop comparing yourself to others. Focus on your one thing. I know that there is a very good reason for your organization to exist. Find that reason. Yes, your mission may be difficult to explain, or it may be a disease that no one has ever heard of, or it may be complicated research. Can you boil your purpose down to one sentence? Why do you exist? What are you trying to change? Who are you serving and why do they need help?

- Frame your message. Add detail to this purpose to make it a message. Frame this message in terms of loss—What would we lose if you closed your doors? What would society lose? What would your clients lose? You may have to work harder to convey this important message to people, to get them to listen. But that's ok. That's your job.

- Use analogies and metaphors to clarify complex issues. These writing techniques help the lay person understand and make sense of new ideas, by comparing it to something familiar to them.

- Add in storytelling. Storytelling is the heart and soul of any nonprofit communications program, and the fuel that powers social media. Collect and tell simple stories or "mission moments" that exemplify and show your purpose.

- Get in front of a group of people who care, even if it's just a small group. (Do not worry about those who don't and will never care. You aren't talking to them.) Encourage this small group of believers to share your mission with five others who could be believers as well.

- Curate a vision board on social media. Your vision board would represent the future that you seek to create. For example, an organization helping sex trafficking survivors could create a vision board with images focused on safety, love, home, and support. Make it public and encourage supporters to add to the vision board.
- Examine your advantages. Niche audiences often require less information because they are familiar with the topic. They also tend to be more vocal. Survey your current supporters to find out what motivated them to get involved with you.
- Address any obstacles to participation. Consider any real or imagined obstacles that people might have to participate in your work or to take an action on your behalf. See if you can address these obstacles in your content:
- Do people not understand what you do?
- Are there lingering stereotypes about your work or the people that you serve?
- How can you address knowledge gaps and misconceptions?
- Can you make the impact of their participation easy to understand—"With your help, we were able to feed 25 families this year."

If you can't find any outsiders who care enough to support you and share your impact with their networks, then you do have to do some real soul searching about how to move forward and why you are doing this work. Most of the social change work done in the world is not as universally appealing as kids and puppies. But that doesn't mean that you shouldn't try. Your cause needs you, and there are people out there ready to hear your message, as long as you are ready to share it.

Our mission is hard to explain.

When a mission is complicated and hard to explain to a lay person, the Curse of Knowledge rears its ugly head. The Curse of Knowledge is when you know a lot about something and you can't imagine what it is like NOT to know it. You don't remember a time when you DIDN'T know it, so it's hard for you to relate to others that do not know as much as you do.

I find myself in this predicament often, and I have to catch myself. The Curse of Knowledge rears its ugly head more frequently when I am teaching others how to best use social media to accomplish their goals. Often, I have to back myself up and start over with the very basics, when I assume I can just jump to creating videos and digital storytelling campaigns. I get excited about my new idea, and I assume that everyone else is on the same page and just as enthusiastic as I am!

The benefits of knowledge can also be a curse. So how can you overcome the Curse of Knowledge and communicate about your complex mission effectively? Here are some ideas:

- Lose the jargon. Lose the buzzwords and the industry speak. A regular lay person not in the trenches won't understand what you are talking about, and the message will immediately get lost. Speak your audience's language! Use their search terms, their slang, their language—not what you *think* they should be using, or what you want them to use.

- Spell out everything. Have you ever been on a conference call or in a lecture where an acronym is used that you don't know, and it's never spelled out? Drives me nuts! Explain all acronyms before you use them. In fact, try to explain all the terms that you are using, even if you think they are very elementary. (Imagine if you'd never heard of Twitter and someone started talking about tweeting?)

- Do not assume anything about your audience. For my line of work, this means never assuming that they know how to login to Facebook or that they know the meaning of the word hashtag. This is not meant to be insulting—I have conducted social media workshops with complete beginners that don't know the lingo, but they are more enthusiastic and willing to learn than the tech professionals.

- Don't "dumb down" your presentation. When I say "spell it out" and "don't assume anything" I don't mean make your audience members feel like kindergartners. Start with a baseline and see where your audience is—if it turns out they are more advanced than you anticipated, go from there. Always be flexible.

- Depending on what you are teaching or explaining, don't be condescending or patronizing to your audience. Make your community feel comfortable. There is nothing wrong with being a newbie willing to learn—in fact, it's the job of your nonprofit to educate people on the issue at hand.

- Have patience. Be empathetic and try to put yourself in your community's shoes. When I teach people how to use social media, they are often embarrassed about their lack of knowledge (although they needn't be) and concerned that they are asking "dumb" questions (they never are). Be sensitive to the emotions that your audience is feeling and use patience when answering questions.

In the same vein of complicated missions and complex programming—How can a nonprofit create compelling social media content when they don't provide direct services? What if your organization focuses on advocacy and research? How can you pull heartstrings and connect with donors without these direct services stories?

The good news! You can. Here are two ways:

- Paint a picture of the future—if you win. Lay out for your online community what would happen if your vision of the future was realized. If you accomplished your mission, if you achieved your goals, if you were all able to go home happy, and if you solved the problem that you set out to solve. What does that look like? Feel like? Smell like? How does the staff feel? How do others feel?

- Tell a story about the future—if you lose. Describe, with evocative and descriptive language, the future if you were forced to close your doors today. What would be lost? Who would suffer? What would happen? Paint me a picture of this future—the one without you in it. You may not be able to point directly to testimonials and success stories, but think creatively about the way in which your work impacts people. And I promise you, it does!

We are worried about trolls and haters.

When I speak with nonprofits about their biggest fear in using social media, most say to me that they are scared of negative feedback and online "haters" or people who will say bad things about them publicly.

Many nonprofits seem to think that all the online wack jobs, former staff members, and disgruntled clients will come out of the woodwork and vent on their Facebook walls, tweet bad things about them, and write nasty comments on their blog. It's important to realize that these occurrences, for small nonprofits especially, are rare. But whether or not your nonprofit is active on social media, your community is out there in the world, discussing your work, debating the issue, and talking about your nonprofit. So while you can't control the conversation, you can be made aware of what's being posted, and attempt to steer the discussions in the right direction.

Here's how to counter your nonprofit's fear of negative social media comments:

- Refer back to the internal and external social media policies you created in Chapter 7, Growing an Organizational Culture that Embraces Social Media. If you have set policies in place, monitoring comments will not seem arbitrary, as you will have rules to guide you.

- Jump right in. Get in the conversation. Start using social listening tools to see what is being said, positive or negative, about your organization and your issue. In my experience, the majority of nonprofits never experience direct confrontation or conflict on their Facebook walls and Twitter feeds.

- Embrace the haters, if you have any. If you are working towards a mission that is controversial and polarizing, such as LGBTQ rights or abortion rights, expect the nay-sayers to comment. Be prepared for their vitriol and their attacks, and respond in a professional, educated way—school them with facts and kill them with kindness. Always be gracious, but delete and block those who directly violate your social media policies.

- Seize the opportunity to shine. Use any negative feedback or comments that you get as an opportunity to respond in an eloquent way. Show the world how you respond to criticism—it speaks volumes about your organization's culture and character.

- Learn. Use comments and feedback gathered from social media as a way to improve your services and programs. Conversations, discussions and debates around your cause and your mission are happening online right now. Your constituents, donors and supporters are involved in these conversations, whether or not you are there participating. You need to think about how your organization can insert itself in a way that helps move the needle forward.

- Train staff on ways to have difficult conversations online. For example, the progressive online community Uplift provides online training on how to have persuasive conversations about abortion care. Model appropriate behavior on social media yourself. There are no hard and fast lines anymore between the personal and professional on these platforms. Demonstrate productive uses of social media.

We have zero budget for marketing.

I get it. Lack of marketing capacity is a huge obstacle to creating impact, and it should come as no surprise, since many nonprofits fear paying "too much for overhead" and thus get caught up in a dangerous starvation cycle.

Examples of this marketing starvation cycle can be found almost everywhere. The popular nonprofit fundraising blog The Agitator posted a review of my book *Storytelling in the Digital*

Age: A Guide for Nonprofits. One reader commented on the post, "Would like to get Julia's book, but Amazon's $38.73 price is out of my nonprofit range."

I felt terrible reading that statement, but the reality is this: If your nonprofit does not have $38.73 to spend on a resource that will help you communicate your mission in a more compelling way and fundraise more efficiently, than what does that say about your potential to create impact?

Nonprofits tend to think that all social media is "pay to play"—that is, you can't make an impact without paying for advertising, shelling out for professional photos, and investing in video production. The truth is that social media marketing can be done on a shoestring, using some creativity and your new media studio—your smartphone.

Here are three ways to do it:

- Use your smartphone to take videos. Taking a good video with your phone requires clear sound, a steady hand, and bright lighting. Prop the phone up on a desk in your office and record, or go outside to use the natural light. The key to a good DIY video is to make sure that ambient noise is kept to a minimum. Carefully lay out and practice what you want to say, putting the most important points at the very beginning of the video. Then just hit record!

- Use mobile apps to repurpose photos and video clips you already have. All of the best social video apps let you pull in video clips from your smartphone, and combine them with existing photos or media. You can even create video collages from static photos. The AEIOU Foundation creates simple donor thank you videos using Animoto, using existing program photos looping over stock music (available in the app).

- Use your smartphone to take and edit photos. While it's important to have high-quality, professional photos on your website, on social media, amateur photos can really work. Authenticity is paramount on social media. Photos are a fantastic way to show, and not tell people about your impact. There are a slew of free desktop and smartphone tools out there to edit and enhance your existing photos, or to help you take better photos to showcase your work.

What gets budgeted for gets done—especially in the nonprofit world! Even allocating $20 for a Facebook Ad to promote your annual fundraising gala, the one that you spend thousands of staff hours on, can have a big impact. Put your money where your mouth is. If you say you want to try online fundraising this year, or crowd-funding, or social media marketing, put aside some money to explore new tools and get some professional help implementing them.

My best recommendation for the resource-stretched nonprofit marketing professional is to start very small and grow. Build a community on one channel, then tackle another. Use what you have and mold it for different platforms and channels to get the most mileage out of it.

Activity: On the Social Media Blueprint, write down three of your biggest challenges in using social media effectively at your nonprofit. Then brainstorm two actionable solutions to each challenge.

CHAPTER 18

Why You Should Embrace Your "Slacktivists"

The word "slacktivism" has surfaced so much of late that I feel the need to write a defense of the misunderstood term. Malcolm Gladwell, one of my favorite authors and thought leaders, scoffed at using social media for social change in a famous 2010 piece for *The New Yorker*: Comparing Facebook activism to the civil rights movement, he writes, "In other words, Facebook activism succeeds not by motivating people to make a real sacrifice but by motivating them to do the things that people do when they are not motivated enough to make a real sacrifice. We are a long way from the lunch counters of Greensboro."

"Slacktivism" is loosely defined as taking a simple online action that doesn't lead to so-called "real" participation, like making a donation. Actions may include sharing a post, signing a petition, or tweeting a link to a charity's website.

Often cited as an example of "slacktivism" is the success of the ALS Ice Bucket Challenge (even though hundreds of millions were raised for ALS research). I participated in the challenge, and continue to believe that it created a big opportunity for the sector to examine the way it communicates and reaches out to new supporters.

Opponents of social media campaigns like the Ice Bucket Challenge worry that the nature of the challenge is simply driven by peer pressure and there is no real substance behind participating. I counter that while pouring a bucket of ice water on your head will certainly not cure ALS, it exposes the disease to more people, and raises money for a cure. Having everyone you know, and the celebrities you like participate, piques your curiosity, and even if you don't end up participating, you at least learn a little bit about the cause and the campaign. Even more importantly, we get to see our friends, family, and colleagues giving to charity—this helps to make charitable behavior and participation a normal and desirable behavior, and maybe even cool.

UNICEF Sweden, in a controversial ad campaign, features a poverty-stricken child in a heart-wrenching video, saying, "My mom got sick, but I think everything will be alright. Today UNICEF Sweden has 177,000 likes on Facebook. Maybe they will reach 200,000 by summer." (Rather ironically, they posted this video on social media site YouTube.) The point of the UNICEF campaign is to somehow demonstrate that the people who Like them on Facebook do not eventually give them money. Whether or not UNICEF has thoroughly researched this connection is not discussed. To watch the video, go to www.jcsocialmarketing.com/socialmediabook

I have worked with many nonprofit organizations on their social media strategies. They have dedicated many hours to connecting with stakeholders, engaging community members, and educating the public about their cause and their impact on the world. Attacks on so-called "slacktivists" (anyone who takes an online action on behalf of a nonprofit) are harmful for several reasons:

- It encourages the unhelpful, unproductive, and antiquated nonprofit notion that spending time and money on social media is a waste of time. When done strategically and with purpose, connecting with a fan base and engaging directly with stakeholders is NEVER a waste of time.

- This cynical view minimizes the reality that more and more charities are effectively using social media tools to advocate, raise awareness and, yes, raise money for their causes.

- It's misguided. How do they know that people who take action online don't actually donate money or time to nonprofit causes? Where is this shown with actual, hard data? In fact, there is hard data to disqualify this point of view. The 2018 Global Trends in Giving Survey found that 29% of donors worldwide say that social media is the tool that most inspires them to give; however, email is a close second at 27%. Of those donors inspired by social media, 56% say that Facebook inspires them the most; 20% say Instagram; and 13% say Twitter. Get the full report at www.nptechforgood.com

- Social media efforts cannot exist in a silo. Ideally, they should exist hand-in-hand with the marketing, fundraising, community services, human resources and programmatic efforts of the entire organization. Therefore, social media cannot solely be blamed for a lack of giving or a lack of community participation in a nonprofit's work.

- This patronizing and dismissive attitude towards "slacktivists" assumes that all nonprofit marketing, social media or otherwise, should be 100% focused on the bottom line of raising money.

- Browbeating, guilt mongering, and shaming someone into giving a donation may work once or twice, but it is not a sustainable fundraising strategy. It certainly doesn't inspire pride and a sense of community with the nonprofit. This approach undoubtedly contributes to the data showing abysmal donor retention rates in recent years.

- Where does it stop? Do we criticize people who give us their email address, right before we email them for a donation? Do we sneer at volunteers who give of their time, if they don't give us a sizable monetary contribution?

Yes, it is true, Facebook Likes do not directly save children's lives. (Neither do those posters or that video you created, UNICEF, but that's besides the point.) Effective marketing and fundraising is about telling a story and showing the donor the impact their contribution will have on a cause that they care passionately about.

Building a true community relies on evoking positive emotions—saving children, protecting the environment, building a school—not about creating a shame spiral where your supporters are made to feel badly because they liked you on Facebook.

Part Three

CULTIVATE

"I've learned that people will forget what you said, people will forget what you did, but people will never forget how you made them feel."
—Maya Angelou

What you need to complete this section:
- Your filled out Nonprofit Social Media Blueprint
- The Social Media Calendar template at www.jcsocialmarketing.com/socialmediabook
- Your nonprofit's event calendar for the next three months.

Introduction

Internet entrepreneur Gary Vaynerchuk says, "Make your marketing strategy around attention—nothing else matters." While there is no debate that the ability to grab and keep attention is vital to online community building, I disagree that it's the ONLY marketing strategy you should focus on.

What happens after we grab this attention and raise this awareness? When we are in the business of social change, we have to think beyond just getting the click or the share. What do we do after the initial engagement? How do we bring people further into the fold? How do we nurture this precious attention and make sure we don't squander it? In the last 30 days of this work, we will create a plan to keep up the enthusiasm and momentum, and build on it by enlisting outside support to amplify our message.

In the first two sections we fleshed out your Nonprofit Social Media Blueprint which establishes the infrastructure and framework that will guide our social media efforts. Now we need to start feeding the social media beast—crafting the posts, writing the tweets, recording the videos. The last section of this book will provide you with step-by-step instructions and a calendar to help you efficiently and effectively carry out your daily and weekly social media tasks.

All of the social media pieces will come together into your Social Media Calendar, which will help determine what to post, when to post, and on which platform. We will also review ways to amplify your voice by creating collaborations, recruiting Social Media Ambassadors, and getting started with social media influencers. The last two chapters are focused on measurement, analysis, improvement, building on momentum, and staying productive as a nonprofit social media manager.

Having a fully fleshed out plan, a sense of direction, and some guideposts to steer you along the way, the work of community building on social media becomes much more manageable. Let's review the Nonprofit Social Media Blueprint so far:

- What is your goal—why are you doing the work of social media marketing?
- Who is your audience?
- What is your unique message?
- Which strategies are required?
- Which platforms will best serve your goal and your audience?
- Which tasks are involved?
- What kinds of content will you create—original, repurposed, and curated?
- How will you address social media challenges at your organization?

CHAPTER 19

How to Fill In Your Monthly Social Media Calendar

The Nonprofit Social Media Blueprint guides you as you lay out all of the daily and weekly social media tasks and add them to the Social Media Calendar. Go to www.jcsocialmarketing.com/social-mediabook and access your free Social Media Calendar spreadsheet.

As a nonprofit marketer for a small organization, you wear many hats. Between answering emails, attending meetings, coordinating events, and more, who has time to maintain more than one social media account? I'm here to tell you that you DO have the time. I promise. The answer to managing it all lies in one word—*planning!*

The best way to manage all the moving pieces, content types, and assorted tasks required in an effective social media marketing plan is through a Social Media Calendar. Here are just three reasons to create and maintain a Social Media Calendar for your organization:

- To get a bird's eye view of organizational priorities, and plan a month or more of social media posts.
- To effectively sync social media with any other fundraising or marketing communications that go out during the week.
- To avoid that middle-of-the-day dread when you have yet to post to Facebook or send a tweet.

Let's get started by determining the cadence and frequency of your social media posts, and then we will choose a type of Social Media Calendar that best suits your organization.

How Much Should We Post?

Getting results on social media is similar to creating a plan to increase your fitness, health, and wellness. If you remain committed, focused, and strategic in your workouts and your meal plan, you will get better results than just showing up at the gym for an hour a week or substituting a salad once in a while. How frequently you exercise, how you change your diet, how you structure your day and your habits—that all has a direct affect on your fitness results. Your expectations of your results need to match the time, effort, and resources that you are able and willing to put in. Organizations that bake social media into their work and spend targeted time building their communities are going to get better results than organizations that show up once per week and post something half-baked and mediocre (or worse).

One thought you may have is: "Post daily? But what if we annoy our supporters? I certainly don't want to hear from every organization and business that I follow several times per day." I'm here to assure you that for the majority of nonprofits, especially the smallest ones, this fear of "annoying our supporters with too much communication" is misled, due to the nature of social media algorithms and everyone's extremely busy lives.

The odds are that you will not appear so much that you annoy your social media followers. To understand why this is, you need to understand how social media algorithms work. As an example, every MINUTE on Facebook, users post 510 comments, 293,000 status updates, and 136,000 photos. An average of 4.75 billion pieces of content are shared daily on the network!

If your Facebook Page fans have been using the site for a number of years, imagine the sheer number of friends, businesses, nonprofits, and other pages and profiles they have connected to in that time. There is simply no way, even if a person spends 24 hours a day, seven days a week, on social media, that they will be shown every piece of content and every update possible, from all the people and places to which they are connected.

Another way to assure that you will not annoy your fans and followers is to post content that they actually want to read, watch, and see. I promise that your nonprofit will NOT annoy and turn off your fans and followers IF:

- You are posting things that your audience wants to see.
- You post when you have something interesting and of value to share.
- You are contributing to their lives.
- You remember that all social media posts work best when they are timely and relevant.

If you are doing it right, you will not be irritating. You will be embraced, enjoyed, and celebrated by your online community.

Another important point that I need to make, especially in response to the proliferation of "this is how much to post on social media" articles online, is that there is NO ONE SIZE FITS ALL IN SOCIAL MEDIA. Sure, there are best practices and there is data telling you what the average person does online, how much time they spend, and when they log on. While there is no magic answer to this question of how much to post on social media, here are some guidelines based on best practices. *Remember that you do not need to be on each of these channels—consult your Nonprofit Social Media Blueprint to determine which platforms will work best to get your nonprofit closer to your goal.*

Facebook: Facebook wants brand Pages to focus on engagement (likes, comments, shares, clicks, video views). Every post that you share should be designed to get some kind of engagement, even if it's just a simple like or reaction. As a general rule, aim for three–four well-thought-out posts per week, each with a visual attached. Facebook posts are about quality and not quantity.

Twitter: Twitter is all about real-time interaction. There's no limit to the number of tweets that you can and should post daily, provided that you are adding value and sharing helpful resources or interesting, timely information. If Twitter is part of your Blueprint, aim for two–four tweets a day. This can include retweets of other accounts. If your nonprofit has time-sensitive news to share, you can schedule even more throughout the day using platforms like Hootsuite or Buffer. At least a third of the tweets you share need to be tagging other accounts or replying to people and starting conversations.

Instagram: This platform requires eye-catching, colorful, aesthetically-interesting images or video. If your nonprofit has access to great photos and visuals, or interesting ideas for video, then you should aim for two-three weekly posts on Instagram's main news feed. Consistency rules on Instagram—keep up the posting schedule that you know you can stick with, even if it's just once per week. Never throw up a low-quality image just to make sure that you filled your quota.

Instagram and Facebook Stories: Stories on Instagram and Facebook are poised to take over the regular news feeds of both sites in the next year, both in volume of posts and in popularity and engagement. Instagram Stories alone are used by over 500 million people every day, with one-third of the most viewed Stories coming from businesses, brands, and nonprofits. Instagram and Facebook Stories should be updated daily if you enjoy making them and if you have fun behind-the-scenes, entertaining, off-the-cuff content to share. You can connect your nonprofit business account on Instagram with your nonprofit Facebook Page, and cross post Instagram Stories to your Facebook Stories feed for added exposure and visibility.

LinkedIn: LinkedIn is a great platform to build your nonprofit's professional network. Users here do not share photos of their kids, pets, and meals (for the most part)—they share helpful articles, how to videos, and targeted content around their industry. Post on LinkedIn, either from your personal profile or from your nonprofit's Company Page, when you have an important announcement to share, relevant news, educational information or campaigns that are relevant to your audience. Aim for between one–three posts per week.

Rule of Thumb: A good way to find out your ideal posting frequency is to experiment with your weekly schedule. If you start posting more frequently on a platform, but you don't see an increase in engagement after several weeks, then this means that you should focus more on increasing the quality of the posts, rather than the quantity.

Nonprofit Social Media Blueprint: Write down the platforms that you chose in the previous section, and choose a **realistic** weekly posting schedule. You can always add more days later— the key is to start off with a calendar you know can work!

Daily Theme Calendar

There are two main frameworks to choose from when creating your nonprofit Social Media Calendar from scratch, or when adapting an existing calendar. While you can certainly use pen and notepad, poster paper, or a whiteboard, it's a best practice to use a digital calendar, document, or spreadsheet. Digital calendars, like Google Calendar, are easy to edit and change, and can be accessed on mobile devices, laptops, or desktops by multiple users.

If you plan to start out only posting once per day on one or two social networks, then a very simple Social Media Calendar organized around a daily theme may work for your organization. As you get more comfortable on social media, see what works, and hit your stride, you can level up to a more detailed Calendar that incorporates more platforms and more content.

A Daily Theme Calendar features a specific topic theme for each day of the week, as a way to help you get comfortable creating posts and sharing them daily. For example, a local food bank could create content based on these Daily Themes:

- Monday—#NutritionMonday: Share a nutrition tip or current news story about nutrition or nutrition myths.

- Tuesday—#CharityTuesday: A post featuring a community partner or local organization you work with that you want to highlight.

- Wednesday—#WednesdayWisdom: Post a graphic and an inspiring quote that motivates supporters, or relates in some way to the mission.
- Thursday—#TBT or #ThrowbackThursday: Post an old photo of volunteers, staff, clients or an event and ask your fans and followers to guess the date and place.
- Friday—TGIF: Share a fun video or story that captures the human side of your organization and gives your fans a behind-the-scenes glimpse into the work.

To mix it up a bit, look at national cause awareness days, current events, and the daily goings-on at your own organization for inspiration. For one week in October, Wilco Forest Preserve jumps on the popular social media campaign #BatWeek to debunk myths and misconceptions about bats as creepy, predatory, or monstrous. They showcase cute and cuddly videos of bats and highlight the vital role that bats play in our food ecosystem. By leveraging the widely-used hashtag and popular topic, Wilco reaches their target audience (people interested in bats—and they are a devoted bunch!), and builds a passionate online community around educational and entertaining posts.

Keeping a calendar of relevant holidays and online celebrations will help inform your editorial calendar for the year and make sure you don't miss opportunities to spread your message to a wider audience. Once you get the hang of posting and get more comfortable with creating and sharing posts every day, you can move on to a more advanced Social Media Calendar.

Nonprofit Social Media Blueprint: Do some internet research and write down two cause awareness days tied to your nonprofit work. If you have chosen to create your Social Media Calendar

using the Daily Theme model, fill out the table included in the Blueprint.

Platform Calendar

A more detailed Social Media Calendar is required if you are posting across multiple platforms several times per day, as well as incorporating other digital communications work such as publishing blog posts, making website updates, and scheduling email newsletters.

Go to www.jcsocialmarketing.com/socialmediabook and get your free download of the Social Media Calendar to fill out. If you prefer to create your own, here's how to do it using a simple spreadsheet:

1. Start by labeling the columns.

The first column will list the social media and digital channels that you have decided to use over the next three months (Facebook, Twitter, LinkedIn, Blog, Email, Pinterest, etc.) and the next seven columns will list the days of the week. Keep in mind that you do not have to post seven days per week, but in case you have an event over the weekend, or a relevant milestone to celebrate, you want to keep your options open.

2. Configure the rows.

Each cell should represent one post or tweet. Add two Facebook rows if you post twice per day, three Twitter rows if you tweet three times per day, and so on. If you like, add a row for other types of marketing content you create on a weekly basis, such as blogs, email campaigns, and website updates. As previously discussed, when deciding to use any social media tool, the frequency of posts and the number of channels are determined by your Nonprofit Social Media Blueprint.

3. Start adding events.

Look at your nonprofit organizational calendar for two, three, even four weeks out. Make sure you take note of all important events, meetings, trainings, milestones, birthdays, anniversaries, upcoming announcements, community events, etc. This ensures that nothing falls through the cracks and that all events are promoted adequately, well in advance.

4. Add content ideas.

Look at all of the content ideas that you generated in the last section of this book, and wrote down on your Nonprofit Social Media Blueprint. Add these ideas into the Calendar.

Nonprofit Social Media Blueprint: If you have chosen to create your Social Media Calendar using the Platform model, start filling in your spreadsheet with important events and noteworthy dates. Fill out your Social Media Calendar for the next 30 days.

Tips on Managing Your Social Media Calendar

Block out time for content creation. This is the space in your calendar each week to write and design your posts, tweets, graphics, and other content. Review the content types from the previous section and make a list of what you will need to create, to investigate, to flesh out. You can't just post and tweet in a vacuum with no preparation or planning (well, you can, but you won't get very far). You will need to allocate time to collect, craft, and create the content that goes on these platforms.

Remember what it takes to grow your online community and build your movement on social media. It's not just signing in once a week and sending out a tweet. Success requires:

- Showing up consistently and sharing unique content that serves a purpose.
- Finding and curating interesting stuff from other sources that is relevant to your audience.
- Monitoring topics and trends to stay on topic with the issue or cause.
- Regularly interacting with and commenting on other accounts and what they post.
- Answering questions from your audience and direct messages in a timely fashion.
- Acknowledging community members that share your content with their networks and start conversations with you online.
- Keeping track of what has been shared.
- Measuring what works and doing more of it.
- Regularly, reviewing ongoing analysis and planning for improvement.

Block out time for social listening and monitoring. Look at what others in your industry are posting, what your partners are saying, and what hashtags and news articles are trending.

Schedule time for responsiveness. Schedule time each week (or each day) to respond to questions and comments from your community. Be responsive and accessible. If your online community engages and asks questions, answer them promptly. If you need to wait to get the answer, let them know you will get back to them as soon as you can. 24 hours is an eternity in the social media realm—do your best to respond immediately to comments, questions and feedback on your posts. By showing you are accessible and eager to help, you are setting yourself apart from the social media Ghost Towns—Facebook pages and Twitter accounts that are created but never (or very rarely) maintained.

Use social media automation tools sparingly. I know what you're asking: "Can't we just automate everything to save time?" The short answer is no. Community and movement building do not happen via automated posts and tweets.

Sure, you can schedule posts and tweets strategically and carefully, but do not rely on social media scheduling tools as a crutch or as a silver bullet just to throw something up and see what sticks. Each platform is completely unique, and automating all of your content across platforms doesn't work anymore (not that it worked well even just a few years ago). Beyond character counts, hashtags, and caption lengths, each channel has its own rules, its own best practices, its own etiquette and structure.

Not only that, it has long been demonstrated (but never officially admitted) that social media platforms penalize the reach for content that comes in from outside tools like HubSpot, HootSuite, and Buffer. Continuing to use an outside management tool to automatically populate your social media feeds all the time will cut your reach and decimate potential engagement.

Be flexible. Don't be married to the calendar. It is ok, even encouraged, to go off topic on social media. This will help you engage your supporters, make them laugh, encourage them to share your content and therefore get in front of new people and increase your exposure. Going off topic shows that you are human, that you are not robots, and that you have personality.

If something happens in the news, if there is an exciting development in your field, or if you just want to post about Game of Thrones (because everyone is talking about it), then do it! A couple of off-calendar posts are not going to kill your entire strategy and derail your plan. Being flexible, timely, and human—while having FUN—matters much more than staying 110% on message.

Always refer back to your Nonprofit Social Media Blueprint to guide you. Ask yourself—Is this post or tweet moving me in the right direction? Is it targeted for my audience? Does it match with my goals and with my strategies?

CHAPTER 20

How to Amplify Your Message Through Collaboration (Not Competition)

In a fantastic piece for the *Stanford Social Innovation Review*, community organizing expert Hildy Gottlieb poses the question, "What if we built movements and not organizations?" I'm not suggesting that you throw your org chart in the recycling bin. But I do think that we need to build trusted coalitions and networks of groups, partners, organizations, and others to amplify each other's work and spread noteworthy ideas far and wide.

We need to stop thinking of other nonprofits as competitors. If you are doing mission-driven work and serving a specific community, there should not be another organization like you vying for the same clients and the same supporters. Nonprofits need to shift the conversation from "How can we compete better in our community to get our piece of the pie?" to "How can we collaborate with other organizations that complement our work, and better serve everyone involved?" We should highlight the other groups that make our work possible and that help us accomplish our missions. No nonprofit operates in a void. If we are doing it right, then there is MORE than enough attention—and enough funding—to go around.

Take a look at recent movements that formed around groups passionate about an issue, and not one particular nonprofit brand:

#MarchForOurLives

The March for Our Lives (MFOL) started as a student-led protest and march in support of legislation to prevent gun violence. It continues as a collaboration between Everytown for Gun Safety and student organizers from Never Again MSD, survivors of the mass school shooting that happened in Parkland, Florida in 2018.

#KeepFamiliesTogether

This movement culminated in a series of synchronized marches and demonstrations to protest the Trump administration's family separation policy. Organized by local immigrant rights groups and coordinated via social media, there were over 300 local protests in cities and towns across the US.

#Overcorrection

Investigative journalists at ProPublica partnered with *The Sacramento Bee* and the *Fresno Bee* newspapers to raise awareness of the dangerous conditions in local jails. The three news organizations collaborated to send out a series of co-written tweets around the issue and drive attention to their individual news coverage of the issue.

#GivingTuesday

The GivingTuesday movement was birthed at the 92nd Street Y in New York, but you won't see their logo on the promotional materials or the social media graphics. GivingTuesday was created so that nonprofits across the world could participate in a single day of giving around Thanksgiving, much like brands and retailers leverage Black Friday and Cyber Monday. No one nonprofit owns it, so that it can be adapted and iterated by everyone. Take the examples of the popular campaign #GivingShoesDay led by the nonprofit Dress for Success, and #GivingZooDay, where local zoos and aquariums tweet about animals and the importance of supporting your local institutions.

Collaboration, rather than cut-throat competition, not only benefits the people that we serve but also improves our ability to spread our message. Here are just a few simple ways that your nonprofit can start a marketing collaboration with other like-minded organizations.

First, identify the partners that you want on board. Look at your community, your town or locality, and your region. Ask:

- Who else is working on the same or similar issues?
- Who is working on a problem that is adjacent and related to your mission?
- Who else serves your clients and targets your supporters?

Second, define the parameters of the group. This can be an informal group on Facebook, where nonprofit partners post campaigns and share ideas, or a more formal group that meets in person and is invite-only and exclusive.

Third, invite the group members in, and determine if the group will meet virtually or in-person, or some combination of both. Always explain the reason for forming the group, and give instructions on how to participate.

Here is an example of an invitation email that a nonprofit could use when forming this idea-sharing group in the community:

Dear Betsy,

My name is Julia Campbell, and I am the Director of Development for Super Awesome Nonprofit. We met at the local bank event, and I would love to learn more about your work and your mission. I am forming a nonprofit collaborative for local folks interested in hearing more about each other's impact as well as actively promoting each other on social media channels. The intention is to get more visibility for all of us in the community. I firmly believe that a rising tide lifts all ships, and I would love to have you on board to learn more about your organization, and to help set the direction and priorities of the group.

As Michael Silberman of MobLab writes, "Sharing power and influence isn't easy, but social change organisations that cling to hierarchy and staff-led campaigning are likely to wither when millions of people are embracing new leadership models that emphasise collaboration, transparency, and co-creation."

Nonprofit Social Media Blueprint: List two organizations that you could contact to share their content to your audience, and to ask them to share your content with their audience.

CHAPTER 21

How to Build a Social Media Ambassador Program

We know that public trust in institutions is faltering. People have limited trust in brands, companies, nonprofits, and governmental organizations. However, many people do still overwhelmingly trust their networks of friends, family, and colleagues.

Recommendations and referrals from trusted networks are eminently more powerful than the most exquisitely-designed and well-funded social media advertising campaign. Skepticism around brand promotions and advertising, combined with the sheer amount of information competing for our attention and our wallets, mean that it's time to consider creating a Social Media Ambassador program at your nonprofit. Here are just six reasons why your nonprofit should consider implementing a Social Media Ambassador program.

1. WOM (word-of-mouth) has been proven to work.

Digital marketing expert Jay Baer found that 92% of consumers trust user-generated content and word-of-mouth suggestions more than advertising. One e-commerce study showed that 71% of people are more willing to purchase an item based on social media referrals from friends and family.

The reality is that people do tend to have a high level of trust for word-of-mouth marketing messages. Building a Social Media Ambassador program is the perfect way to give regular people the resources and tools to spread the word about your nonprofit and its work.

2. It's more cost effective than trying to engage complete strangers.

Nonprofits seem to have this view that if they shout very loudly from billboards, flyers, mailers, and social media ads, somehow their message (even if poorly written or thought out) will "cut through the clutter" and delight an entirely new audience of people.

The truth is that no one wants to be interrupted online or offline. No one wants their attention stolen. No one wants to see more advertising, no matter how beautifully designed.

People DO want to hear stories and consume information that is relevant to their lives, their values, and their motivations. Leveraging your existing network of supporters, people who have raised their hand and said "Yes, I am interested!" is much easier and more effective than yelling at strangers to pay attention.

3. You can't launch from scratch.

No matter how elaborate, expensive, or sexy your social media marketing campaign is, if you don't have an audience built up that is interested in seeing it, it will fail. Small nonprofits without large lead generation or supporter acquisition budgets are at a significant disadvantage, because they often have smaller online communities to draw from.

Having a social media ambassador program at your nonprofit will allow you to build a community of raving fans the RIGHT way—holistically and organically. Sure, you can purchase $10K worth of Facebook fans—but they aren't real people and at the end of the day they will do nothing for your bottom line.

The best bet is to start small, work with a focused group of Ambassadors willing to help you share your best content and your most compelling stories, and build an audience online before launching your campaign.

4. They will give you honest feedback.

Social Media Ambassadors will either be familiar with or willing to learn more about your organization, and by design, will end up as some of the most passionate people involved with your cause. These are the kinds of people that you want to attract and retain!

The only way to get more of them into the fold is to understand what motivates them and what information they are interested in. You can use your Social Media Ambassadors as a focus group to test new ideas, share unique stories, and try out experimental content before releasing it to the public.

Not only will the Ambassadors appreciate being part of an exclusive club that gets a first look at your content, they will have a unique perspective on it and will be able to provide you with invaluable, immediate feedback.

5. They will give you new ideas.

Beyond using the Ambassadors as a focus group to provide feedback, actively cultivate their ideas and ask for their thoughts! Ask them about trends that they are seeing in the digital landscape, in the region, and around the issue you are working on.

Social media ambassadors are likely to participate on several different channels, and they can function as your eyes and ears in the field. Have a question about the utility of Snapchat for marketing? Ask the ambassadors for their ideas!

Want to promote your next event? Solicit ideas from the ambassadors as to which channels may be most effective and what messages will resonate. They will most likely come up with great things you hadn't even thought of!

6. Relationships will deepen and strengthen.

Who is more likely to become a loyal supporter and raving fan of your organization—the person who has volunteered to share information about your organization, or the online stranger who may or may not even be remotely interested in your cause?

Rather than putting your focus on casting the widest net possible on the interwebs in the hopes of catching a handful of random eyeballs, why not deepen ties with your current community members? Creating a vibrant and dynamic social media ambassador program at your nonprofit will help you strengthen relationships with the most important people in your network—the ones who are willing to put their reputations on the line to share information about your work.

They are affirming their shared identity with you by their willingness to help you raise your visibility and bring more people into the fold. This special group may know you, they make like you, but if you give them a great experience and make them feel valued and useful, they will love you.

Step 1–Identify.

Social Media Ambassadors have the potential to elevate your results, if you know where to find them, how to recruit them, and how to coordinate and energize them. So, where can you start to look for these wonderful people?

Your email list. Determine who is opening your email newsletters and communications, who is sharing the content, and who is forwarding the emails to their networks.

Your social networks.

- Use LinkedIn Groups strategically to find people who care about your cause and who are vocal online. You can now search LinkedIn profiles for Volunteering History and Causes.

- On your Facebook Page, you can see who is liking, commenting on, and sharing your content—thank them profusely and get them on your email list.

- Twitter is a perfect place to engage with supporters. See who is following you and how active they are on the site. Create a Twitter list of all the Twitterers who have shared your content and mentioned you.

Your co-workers and organization volunteers. Who is always sharing information about your work? Who happens to love social media and digital technology? Look at the group of people that surround you every day. They have the passion, the knowledge, and the behind-the-scenes perspective—some of them would undoubtedly make fantastic Social Media Ambassadors.

Your donors, event attendees, and peer-to-peer fundraisers. The people who come to all of your events, and the special group that raises money for you during walks, marathons, fashion shows, and more. Make a list of these influential people in your network that would make great Social Media Ambassadors.

Step 2–Recruit.

The best way to recruit someone to be a Social Media Ambassador is to craft a personal solicitation, and to ask them. Provide details on what the work will include, and assure them they can opt-out at any time.

A great way to get people on board is to explain the value of the work. Share with them: "If you join us in this movement and help spread the word on social media, this will result in increased participation, donations, partnerships, and more clients willing to come forward to seek help."

A sample Social Media Ambassador job description is as follows:

"Thank you for your interest in being a Social Media Ambassador! We are so excited to have you on board, and can't wait to get started.

Super Awesome Nonprofit Social Media Ambassadors will:

- Have a passion for the organization and a willingness to spread the word about the organization far and wide;
- Actively participate in forming and carrying out the story-telling strategy of the organization by providing feedback and ideas;
- Keep an eye and an ear out for great stories that can be shared about our work;
- Follow, fan, and like the organization on our social media platforms;

- Share one tweet or Facebook post per week;
- Post graphics to your social networks (we will provide the graphics);
- Invite others in your network to become involved."

Feel free to add your own wording and your own requirements—make it fun and light! This is not the place to include lengthy legal policies and restrictions. You want your Social Media Ambassadors to be the source of enthusiasm, passion, and ideas.

Greenpeace calls their ambassadors the "Social Media Hive," fighting for "a green and peaceful future." In the About section on their website, they list the reasons for creating this program, and have explicit instructions on how to join and participate. They also manage a Facebook Group with over 300 members that they can activate when they have a campaign to promote.

Social Media Ambassadors at the State College of Florida Foundation are asked to regularly share content from the College's social media accounts and to promote time-sensitive initiatives and programs.

Watts of Love, a nonprofit that provides safe, sustainable lighting sources for those living without access to electricity, promotes their Social Media Ambassador program as a great resume and personal brand builder. You must apply to be a part of it, and they list the Ambassadors on their website and give them exclusive access to events, raffles, and other contests. When you sign up, they email several times per year, including sample posts and helpful tips on how to leverage social media to showcase their mission and raise money for the cause.

Make it a movement that works better when more people are involved. That's the secret to the success of social media—it only works if everyone uses it. How can your movement express the ways in which this is better if everyone is involved?

Have a scheduled Google Hangout or Zoom/Skype call to welcome in the Social Media Ambassadors. Give a quick intro to the job and tasks. Share an impactful story. Walk through any pertinent information that they may need and where to find it. Most importantly, be excited!

Create a private Facebook Group, LinkedIn Group, or email listserv for the Ambassadors. This group is meant to share information, get feedback, and solicit new ideas. Encourage interaction in this group, along with Q&A and feedback. Bonus points for posting video or hosting livestream broadcasts inside the group to give updates on progress and celebrate accomplishments!

Step 3—Make it easy.

Make it extremely easy to share your nonprofit's content on social media. You can encourage commenting and other interactions by disabling strict privacy settings on your social media sites. Another way is to add social share buttons to all website content and email communications.

Write the updates for the Social Media Ambassadors that they can simply cut, paste, and share. Create graphics and share photos with the Ambassadors. When writing these posts, be thoughtful and strategic. This works better: "Hey Storytelling Ambassadors! Please tweet this! The @waterforlife campaign for fresh water is well underway—can you donate $1 to help a child now? #waterforall" vs. "Hey everyone, please tweet about our fresh water campaign today!"

Most importantly, let your Social Media Ambassadors determine how they want to share the information. Provide updates in several social media formats to let the online supporters choose where they want to share. It's not about where you want them to share the information (although you can suggest it); it's about where they are going to want to post it! They are in control of the where and the when, and you are in control of the why.

The Massachusetts Conference for Women Social Media Street Team promotes the mission and the activities of the Conference committee year-round, and ramps up activity in the weeks leading up to the Conference in Boston. They send out weekly emails with tweets, Facebook and LinkedIn posts, Pinterest pins and Instagram ready photos, with all the graphics provided, hashtags provided, and all speakers and relevant people tagged. The Team coordinator makes it very easy to cut, paste, and share on social media channels, increasing participation by lowering the barrier.

Susan G. Komen Florida partnered with video software company CauseVid to collect stories from potential Social Media Ambassadors on their website. Using a simple form, they asked the question: *Why is ending breast cancer important to you? With your help, we're having a real impact against breast cancer. Record your video and join us in ending breast cancer forever.* Ambassadors recorded a short video and were asked to share it with others on social media. Komen Florida also provides virtual Ambassador Badges, that their social media team members can add to their blogs, social media accounts, and websites.

Step 4—Mobilize with clear instructions.

Give frequent updates to your Ambassadors to let them know what's coming, what's on the horizon, and how you may seek their help. If you are looking to get a specific number of signatures on a petition, update your online supporters on your progress! Celebrate milestones in fundraising—"We've raised $5,000—only $5,000 more to go!" People love to be part of success.

Social Media Ambassadors are online and always looking for content to share with their networks. They support you and your cause already. They are most likely looking for easy ways to get more involved. Give them easy instructions and compelling content and see your online reach explode!

Step 5—Acknowledge and thank.

Be sure to acknowledge and thank your Social Media Ambassadors regularly. I recommend organizing a "thank you" campaign using online videos to show them you are grateful for their work. Hand-written, offline thank you notes are always unexpected and appreciated.

If appropriate and if you can, give the Ambassadors something special for participating. Make them feel like they are part of something exclusive and special! This could mean holding a special cocktail hour before your gala just for the Ambassadors, or sending them chocolates, stickers, anything extra and out of the ordinary.

Be sure to continue to show the Ambassadors the impact of their work. Beyond the recognition and the gifts, this is the most important step. Your online supporters want to know that all their tweeting, Facebook posting and blogging have actually helped your organization. Otherwise, why waste their time?

Remember, be open-minded and don't get discouraged. Not everyone will be a Social Media Ambassador (no matter how much you want them to). Also, just because someone is influential online, or seems like a great fit on paper, does not mean that your cause will resonate with them.

In order to keep momentum, actively look everywhere for people who are passionate about your cause. Cultivate your current online advocates and thoughtfully create others. Identify and acknowledge the special people. See what you can do to find your offline community and entice them to join you online.

Crossroad Child & Family Services in Fort Wayne, Indiana, created a Social Media Ambassador program to raise money on Giving Tuesday. They mobilized the Ambassadors by creating a job description, emailing them three times before Giving Tuesday with instructions and reminders, and relying on them to post on Facebook during the fundraising campaign.

The National Osteoporosis Foundation (NOF) activates their Brand Ambassadors to:

- Advocate on behalf of their cause to congressional leaders.
- Direct people to the NOF website to download advocacy tools and resources.
- Pass along key research and updates.
- Respond to community conversations about industry news and events related to the disease, both offline and online.

More examples of nonprofit Social Media Ambassador programs can be found at www.jcsocialmarketing.com/socialmediabook.

Nonprofit Social Media Blueprint: List five people to be Social Media Ambassadors. Draft a three-sentence job description to share with them.

CHAPTER 22

How To Create a Social Media Toolkit

In order to make the work easy and fun, provide your Social Media Ambassadors with a toolkit of free and accessible resources that they can use to spread the word. Include all relevant information in one place, ideally on your website, where others can also use it to show their support of the cause.

Some crucial items to include in your Nonprofit Social Media Toolkit include:

A short intro video summarizing how to use the Toolkit. Never assume that your fans and followers understand how best to use social media, or even how to prioritize all the great information in the Toolkit. Take a 30 second-one minute video with your smartphone to say thank you, and let them know how to use the Toolkit. For example: What are some of the best practices in sharing on Facebook, Instagram, and Twitter? What are the most important messages, stories, and facts to highlight?

Creating and posting an intro video for people who access your Toolkit will make SUCH a difference, and I guarantee it will set you apart from other organizations who simply put up a ton of information but don't expressly give guidance on how to use it.

Updated data and statistics on the problem you are solving. Stories are the most important item to share because they play to human emotions and encourage us to get involved, but data and statistics on the problem are also good. Prove that you are solving a timely problem that would only get worse without your nonprofit. Show me what would happen if you closed your doors tomorrow. Demonstrate that you are answering a call and addressing a real need in the community.

Video files that people can download and share. Do not simply upload all of your videos to YouTube and share links from there. Each social media site is its own country, with its own etiquette, language, and culture. Uploading a video file directly into Facebook (also called on demand or native video) dramatically increases reach and engagement. Encourage supporters and ambassadors to directly upload the video file into their social media profiles, with attribution linking back to your organization.

Testimonials and success stories from people who have been transformed by your work.

Storytelling works best when soliciting funds, online or offline. In an online fundraising campaign, one story should be the centerpiece of the entire campaign. However, it's great to have more stories to share, either on your blog or somewhere on your website, for added social proof. On their website, the Denver Rescue Mission has an entire section called Stories of Changed Lives. "Being pregnant on the street was terrifying," Donna says as she begins to share her story. "I wondered every day if I would lose the baby. I was constantly stressed. I even slept in my car for a few weeks before I was humbled enough to ask for help from anyone." These stories are collected all in one place, and made easy to share via links on social media.

List of relevant hashtags to include in social media posts. Hashtags are useful ways to get your content found by more people interested in the same topic, but your supporters may not know which hashtags to use. Including a small list of suggested hashtags will save time and ensure that your online fundraising campaign content gets seen by more eyeballs.

Approved photos for distribution (perhaps with your logo or watermark). Visuals are everything on social media. Video works best, and photos are next in line—the king and queen of engaging social media content. Often, a wonderful photo is worth 1000 words. Include a variety of photos for your supporters to download and share so they don't have to search around on your site, or go to Google Images and get pictures that they do not have permission to use. You should also include high resolution logos for your nonprofit.

Blog post ideas and templates. There may be members of your online community that want to blog about your nonprofit and your online fundraising campaign, but they don't know where to start. Give them as many ideas as possible for potential blog posts to help jumpstart their creativity.

Graphics to use on social media (profile images, cover photos). Create some inspiring quotes or other graphics that can be shared on social media. Use apps like Canva or WordSwag for easy creation and social media optimization.

Sample outreach email copy that Ambassadors can cut, paste, and personalize. Personalized emails always work best, but if your supporters are short on time, provide them with a short and to-the-point email about your online fundraising campaign and why it's important. Encourage people to include their own voice and language in the email.

FAQs about your organization and your cause. Which questions do you always get from your stakeholders, clients, staff, volunteers? Limit the FAQ to no more than five bullet points. Be sure to address myths and misconceptions that go along with your cause or your organization, as well as stereotypes about the population that you serve, and why it is important to support your nonprofit right now.

Sample pre-written tweets, Facebook posts, LinkedIn posts, etc. that people can cut and paste. Write the tweets out ahead of time to ensure that they don't exceed the character limit and that all relevant accounts are tagged properly. Same goes with Facebook and LinkedIn posts, and any other type of content you want people to just grab, cut, and paste onto their social accounts. The easier that you can make this process, the better!

Social Media Tip Sheet for newbies. Some of your ambassadors and supporters may never have shared information like this on their social media accounts before, and they may need a little bit of a primer. I suggest sharing your own internal and external social media policies with them, and providing them with a lot of encouragement. Always explain the rationale behind the Social Media Toolkit and share some examples of how social media can be used to really drive engagement and donations for nonprofits.

The nonprofit Road Scholar provides in-depth international learning trips for solo travelers or couples, usually over the age of 60. They organized an awareness and engagement campaign called #AgeAdventurously, with the goal to showcase the photos, videos, and travel experiences of their participants on social media. However, they found that their target demographic, being a bit older, had a few questions about different social media platforms, and how best to use them. In response to this need, they created a blog and video titled "What the Heck is Instagram? Inside the App" that ended up being so popular, they quickly came up with a series around social media:

- "What the Heck is a Hashtag? Social Media Tips for Baby Boomers & Beyond"
- "What the Heck is Spotify? Music to your Ears"
- "What the Heck is Pinterest?"

The result is a win-win—their target audience gets valuable and useful information from the nonprofit, and Road Scholar grows their social media base of advocates.

For real-world examples and links to online nonprofit Social Media Toolkits, go to www.jcsocialmarketing.com/socialmediabook.

CHAPTER 23

How to Connect with Influencers to Spread Your Message

One of the most fantastic benefits of actively participating on social media is that influential people are easier to reach than ever before. By influential, I don't mean huge celebrities like Lady Gaga or Oprah Winfrey. I mean influencers in your own backyard, your town, and your region—people that are influential in your cause space or community.

When I started out, I had no blog readers, no email subscribers, no social media followers. I started from scratch. So I did research on the brands, blogs, and influencers in the space that already had the attention of my target audience—nonprofit marketing professionals.

This led me to relationships with TechSoup, Wild Apricot, Bloomerang, CauseVox, Classy, CharityHowTo, Nonprofit Learning Lab, DipJar, and more. Through social media, you can catch the attention of potential partners and influencers, by @mentioning them on Twitter, posting on their Facebook wall, messaging them on LinkedIn, re-pinning their stuff on Pinterest.

Blackbaud and Small Act created a great infographic describing the four types of social influencers to which your nonprofit needs to pay attention.

First group—Key Influencers. Key Influencers are the well-known names and brands who have a lot of clout within your niche. For the nonprofit space, think Beth Kanter and Vu Le. Key Influencers are directly changing and shifting discussions on certain topics, and can often mobilize their loyal online communities to action with just a simple tweet or post.

I've found that despite their packed schedules, influencers in the nonprofit space are frequently very generous with their influence and willing to help others. The problem is that marketers engage these generous souls only when they want something!

Action item: Create genuine, authentic connections with just a few Key Influencers in your space. Twitter and YouTube are great places to look for influential creators and bloggers, based on keywords and topics. Even just using Google can find you some worthy connections.

Second group—Engagers. This group is opinionated. They are looked at as informed and trustworthy and they generate a ton of posts and tweets. Engagers like connecting people with other people or causes and brands that they may be interested in, and they love sharing and disseminating information.

Action item: Identify who in your network is a top Engager. You can find them by their social network activity, number of tweets and posts and number of connections.

Third group—Multichannel Consumers. Multichannel Consumers engage online but also like offline touchpoints such as phone calls, mailings and events. They require a bit more attention from your organization, because they are not online as much as Engagers and Key Influencers.

Action item: Do not ignore this group! I see too many nonprofits rush into social media without a plan to incorporate the other channels and donor touchpoints. Think about ways you can use social media to augment what you are already doing offline and draw even more people into the fold.

Fourth group—Standard Consumers. The majority of people who participate online are Standard Consumers. They are quietly going about their business, looking at funny cat videos, liking photos of their grandchildren, perhaps sharing something they find interesting or entertaining. They are usually committed to one social network and don't spread themselves too thin.

Action item: Get this group comfortable with your nonprofit and your message. If most of the Standard Consumers who support your nonprofit are on Facebook, then start there. Entertaining and soft information works best for this group, so it is ideal to have a mix of types of posts and content.

Nonprofit Social Media Blueprint: Write down two influencers that you could contact to help spread your message.

How to Get Started With Social Media Influencers

The key to working with influencers is that it needs to be a mutually beneficial relationship. To understand how to work with an influencer, you need to determine what motivates them and how they operate.

You must be authentic—it must come across that you know and like the influencer in question, and that you have read their content. Ideally you would follow them on their social channels, subscribe to their blog and email newsletter, and comment thoughtfully on their videos or other content. You can't be a fair weather fan and then ask them for a favor. This does not work, and it doesn't reflect well on you or your nonprofit.

Start small. I recommend personally contacting five influencers each week and asking them to look at your latest creation that you want shared—your blog, your Twitter feed, your video, your website, whatever it is. Ask them to retweet or share on another channel if they like it and if they think it would benefit their audience. THANK THEM profusely if they oblige. Don't stalk them, and don't be fake. Due to the sheer number of requests that influencers have to sort through, they can smell spam and sales pitches a mile away.

Start a guest blogging initiative. Identify places where you can guest blog. The key to a successful guest blogging initiative is to look at it like forming partnerships. Posting your content on someone else's site must be mutually beneficial for both parties.

Think about what's in it for the site where you are guest blogging. Ideally, the site administrator would get several benefits, including time saved, fresh content, a unique perspective, and something unique and interesting to share with their audience.

What's in it for you and your nonprofit? There are three main benefits to guest blogging:

- More exposure to the audience that you desire to reach
- Enhanced credibility with your audience
- More visibility for your ideas.

Full disclosure, I receive requests to guest blog on my site EVERY SINGLE DAY. Most of these requests are not well thought out, they don't match my audience and my topics, and they sound generic and simply cut-and-pasted. When approaching a blogger, be sure you can explain: a) why you are approaching them specifically and b) how this blog post will benefit their audience.

I'm protective of my audience and I won't share just anything—it has to provide value and be worthy of my audience's attention and time.

Give free webinars. Consider forming partnerships with groups, brands, and companies that already have a large webinar audience and an established platform. Webinar presenters are not just consultants and public speakers! Often the best nonprofit webinars I attend feature nonprofit professionals in the trenches, sharing insights, new approaches, and innovations with the attendees. The key is to find out who has the attention of your target audience, and work with them.

Get on podcasts. Podcasts are exploding in popularity, and they often have dedicated audiences that listen every single week. Often podcast hosts are looking for unique and interesting guests that would appeal to their audience. Some nonprofit podcasts and video shows that you should check out, and potentially pitch your nonprofit to can be found on this collaborative Google doc: bit.ly/nonprofitpodcasts.

Target and reach out to journalists and reporters. Reporters should be targeted the same way as any other potential partner— purposefully and strategically. Do some research. Make sure you are contacting the correct person at the newspaper and media outlet.

Start your email to any reporter with the hook. There MUST be an interesting angle for them to pay attention. Here are three surefire ways to get your email pitch deleted immediately:

- It's boring, not well-written, and doesn't have an interesting story or hook.
- It's been sent to the wrong person (no, they won't forward it).
- It doesn't have a local, relevant angle.

If your nonprofit is active on Twitter, make a Twitter list of reporters that cover stories in your industry, about your cause, and in your local area. Follow them, retweet them, comment on their tweets, and then sell them on your fantastic idea.

Nonprofit Social Media Blueprint: Write down two ways that you are going to reach out to and connect with these influencers.

C H A P T E R   2 4

Quick Guide to Launching a Two-Week Social Media Marketing Campaign

Now that it's all in place, and you've spent some time building up a community, you can launch a dedicated marketing campaign. A social media marketing campaign is complementary to but more laser-focused than your regular, daily social media posting and community-building work. A campaign refers to a concentrated burst of activity, during a set period of time, focused around one call-to-action on social media.

There are four main phases of a nonprofit social media marketing campaign: Planning, Launch, Execution, Follow-Up. I recommend allotting at least one month for the Planning phase; two weeks for the Launch and Execution portion of the campaign; and two weeks for Follow-Up.

Here is a quick guide of the steps required to carry out your two-week social media marketing campaign:

Planning Phase

1) Choose a SMART goal. Your SMART goal will provide the framework of the campaign and will help you determine if it was successful or could be improved in certain areas. You may hit some of the goals and not all of them, and that will give you valuable information on what's attainable going forward.

SMART goals are:

- Specific.
- Measurable.
- Attainable.
- Relevant.
- Timebound.

For Media Literacy Week, I worked with the campaign Digital Age Kids to promote their free curriculum and classroom materials. We launched a two-week awareness campaign targeted at teachers and parents of elementary school students interested in digital literacy and providing expanded opportunities in the classroom. The overarching goal was to raise awareness of the research and offerings of Digital Age Kids, and we broke that down into several SMART goals we could measure during and after the campaign:

- 350 combined downloads of the research paper and the free elementary school curriculum during Media Literacy Week in October.
- 100 website visitors per day during Media Literacy Week.
- Increase in Twitter followers by 25%.

- Increase in retweets on Twitter by 25%.
- Five media inquiries during Media Literacy Week.

Having and sticking to SMART goals will allow you to see if your campaign worked and if it's on track to succeed. If you have never run a social media marketing campaign before, look at overall website traffic and social media numbers, and make an educated guess as to the numbers if there was a dedicated push to increase them. If it's your very first time, work on building up an engaged community on social media first, and then look at their overall participation, involvement, and engagement when creating your campaign SMART goals.

2) Create a compelling campaign theme. Every campaign has a theme that will resonate with a particular audience. Conduct research on successful social media marketing campaigns that you've seen and write down what they have in common. What can you adapt and emulate? What seems to be working? What is unique and interesting?

Then take some time and choose a unique campaign theme. The theme goes beyond a simple hashtag, but that should be considered if planning a mass outreach and engagement campaign. Think about the topics that resonate most with your audience specifically. To get even more ideas, consider forming a small but mighty Campaign Committee to give you feedback, help with the work, and follow-up at the end of the campaign.

After the theme is settled upon, write up a short and pithy campaign pitch. This is a very brief version of a traditional case statement. In two sentences, you should be able to tell me what you are trying to accomplish, why you are trying to accomplish this, and how I can help. If your goal is fundraising, clearly explain why potential donors should give during the campaign. If your goal is engagement, explain why people need to participate, what will it get them, and what the benefit will be to advance the cause in general.

3) Start creating the necessary assets for the campaign. These may include:

- Landing page with your campaign pitch
- Social media cover art
- Social media graphics
- Infographics
- Campaign video
- Blog posts
- Email copy

One Week Out

One week before the campaign launches, tease the campaign on social media and email, announcing that something exciting is coming. Be sure to work with your influencers and Social Media Ambassadors (see previous chapters) to get them to spread the word when you launch.

Finalize all of the written copy and visual assets, and test the website landing page to make sure everything is working and loading fast on mobile devices and desktop.

Launch Phase

The first day of the campaign will have the most buzz and momentum because people love something new. Check in with Committee members, influencers, and Social Media Ambassadors to ensure they are clear about their assignments. Make sure that they can access the Social Media Tool Kit if they need graphics, photos, and resources. Send your launch email—this email is the most crucial. For extra credit, go live on your nonprofit Facebook Page and get people excited about the campaign launch. Shoot a quick Instagram Story with a behind-the-scenes view of the launch. If you use Twitter, tag specific people to make sure they see your tweets.

Execution Phase

Keep up campaign momentum by regularly sharing video and text updates of your progress towards your goal. Let people know what has been accomplished so far, how many people have participated, and what still needs to be done to achieve your goal.

Continue to send targeted, short emails about the campaign. Share your progress and an inspiring story, asking people to participate and/or share with their networks. Check in with the Campaign Committee and Social Media Ambassadors. Answer questions and comments via email and social media.

At the end of the first week of the campaign, post a THANK YOU PARTICIPANTS update on all social media channels, including a graphic, photo, or short video. Take a quick video for Facebook thanking everyone who participated and asking all procrastinators to get on board before the deadline.

During the second week, in the last few days of the campaign, be sure to thank participants on social media via a short video, and let people know that there is still time left to take action before the campaign ends. Send one last email sharing a story and encouraging people to help. Tell your supporters you are humbled and inspired by their participation in the campaign.

Follow Up Phase

When the campaign is over, the excitement doesn't stop there! Have a plan to cultivate the participants in the campaign, whether they signed an email, made a small donation, or just clicked on a link. Hold a virtual meeting with the Campaign Committee for a quick evaluation, and schedule a longer meeting in the coming weeks to review the entire campaign.

Thank the Social Media Ambassadors, the influencers, and the Campaign Committee and ask for their honest and candid feedback, to help you prepare for future campaigns. Let everyone who participated know how it went and THANK them profusely. You will know success if everyone is asking—"That was awesome, what's next?"

Examples of nonprofit Social Media Marketing Campaigns can be found at www.jcsocialmarketing.com/socialmediabook.

Nonprofit Social Media Blueprint: Write down one draft SMART goal that could translate into a two-week social media marketing campaign.

CHAPTER 25

How to Measure Success and Document Results

Don't get me wrong. I think it's fantastic when nonprofits want to measure their social media efforts. In fact, it's vital—consistent measurement is something I strongly recommend (a.k.a. require) of all my clients.

Without measurement and analysis:

- How will you know what to improve upon?
- If you don't know where you want to go, how will you know when you get there?
- How will you know that you have taken the right road?
- How will you know how to get there again, and again?

This brings me to my big problem with the majority of social media measurement tools and spreadsheets. They only measure the numbers of followers, likes, views—also called vanity metrics.

Vanity metrics may make you feel good—"Look, 10 new Twitter followers this week!"—but the numbers alone are not telling the story of progress towards your goal.

Sure, you do want to see a steady increase in those kinds of numbers over time—and you certainly don't want to backslide and lose followers and fans. But, they are not the most important statistics to follow in your quest for social media success. Ask yourself—Are you getting more people to take action on the issue? Are you receiving more inquiries for donations? Are your events well-attended?

To determine what to measure, we need a combination of "vanity metrics" and goal-specific metrics. As Beth Kanter wrote on her blog, nonprofits need to use the "Say So What To Your Data Three Times" principle.

When you see a spike in website traffic or Facebook engagement, ask—So what? Where did the traffic originate from? What are the possible reasons for an increase in engagement?

Find out where the website traffic or increased engagement originated. It may have come as a result of your nonprofit being mentioned in the news, or being retweeted by an influencer, or through sharing a perspective on a trending news story. Ask again—So what?

Did it result in more email sign-ups? Petition signatures? Membership inquiries? Online donations? Did it help you achieve your desired strategies and move you towards your stated goal?

Remember that "raised awareness" in your online community does not automatically translate into action. So how should you measure the real value of social media for community building? Here are a few tips:

1. Go back to the strategies and tasks that you set in your Nonprofit Social Media Blueprint in the first section. The metrics that you measure will help determine the effectiveness of the strategies and tasks you chose.

Strategies	Tasks	Metrics to Measure Effectiveness
(Example) Get people excited about what we do.	(Example) Share a weekly video on Facebook that goes behind the scenes of our work and highlights staff and volunteers. Create graphics and visuals about our work that people can easily share on social.	Blog post traffic Blog subscribers Facebook engagement Facebook followers Facebook referral traffic to website/email sign-ups
(Example) Shed light on the issue in a compelling way.	Share timely news each week on the issue with our commentary and perspective. Share posts that invite discussion and debate from our community.	Video views Video engagement Website traffic Donation page clicks Conversions (how many people clicked on the page and completed a donation)
(Example) Share more inspiring stories.	Share Instagram Stories once per week from the field. Hold a digital storytelling training for staff and board members. Invest in a video series depicting transformational client stories.	Instagram Stories views Instagram engagement Instagram followers Staff collecting stories Staff sharing stories Video views Video engagement

2. Always remember the true value of achieving your goal. The value does not lie simply in increasing the number of Twitter followers or Facebook fans. Dig deeper. The value of achieving success in building a community on social media can be linked to:

- Increased donations and revenue.
- New donor prospects.
- Word-of-mouth goodwill for the organization.
- Ability to hire and train more staff.
- Ability to serve more clients.
- Prestige as a reputable and successful nonprofit organization.
- Greatly enhanced media and community relationships.
- Increased positive coverage in local media.
- Increased community partnerships.

Facebook Likes are nice, but engaging people and getting them to take your desired action is nicer! Keep your eye on the big picture and always dig deeper into your metrics—that will help you find focus on those days when it seems you are spinning your wheels.

Going beyond numbers and quantitative data, there are three qualitative ways to determine nonprofit marketing success, of which social media is certainly a large part:

1. Your fans would put your bumper sticker on their car (or a frame on their Facebook profile).

Car, laptop, Hydroflask, Trapper Keeper—your fans love you so much that they would put your sticker on their most valuable possessions. They would wear your t-shirt, drink from your coffee mug, and use your branded water bottle. Your social media platforms should be cultivating this sense of community.

In the digital space, in lieu of physical bumper stickers, you can create cover art and photo frames for people to use on their profiles. Susan G. Komen Florida offers a variety of Facebook profile frames that supporters can use to show their public support for the cause on social. Save Buzzards Bay is a small environmental protection nonprofit, and they send out physical bumper stickers to their donors, with a digital ask to post them to social media using their hashtag.

There is such power in getting your supporters to brandish your logo in public, showing it off to their networks. This is the way that we identify and showcase to others what we stand for. It's a public declaration of our values and our worldview. It's also the way that we attract like-minded people that stand for the same things. I feel an instant kinship with others who support the same charities. It helps us build our communities, establish our personalities, and make connections online.

2. You aren't afraid of haters.

Haters, trolls on the interwebs—they don't scare you! If your social media work is thriving, you simply brush your shoulders off when you see a negative comment online. You aren't worried about criticism on social media, because you know that your online community has your back.

You have confidence in your community members. They are there for you. They will step up to bat, insert themselves in conversations to set the record straight, and defend you to people who hate on your org, your cause, and your issue. Because an attack on you is an attack on *them*—what they stand for and who they are down to their very core.

3. You feel genuinely proud.

You know that feeling that you can't put your finger on, when things are going well and you feel like you are really doing work that matters? The way to know if your social media marketing is working, or on it's way to really working, is if you feel good about it.

You don't feel slimy. You don't feel evil. You don't feel smarmy, or manipulative, or yucky about the marketing messages you send out. Instead, you feel like you are building something.

The only way to do this is to act like a human, and not a faceless brand. Focus on making real connections, not just pushing out promotions to get a few more clicks. Pride in your work also means that you know you could approach your community with an ask, and they would respond. They would provide feedback. They would open their wallets.

The only true currency on social media is trust and attention, and the only way to get it is through valuable communication that is desired and needed by your online community.

Nonprofit Social Media Blueprint Activity: Write down three metrics you will measure to determine social media success.

CHAPTER 26

How to Stay Productive as a Busy Nonprofit Social Media Manager

"**B**e efficient."

"Keep on task."

"Remain laser-focused."

For a nonprofit social media manager, those phrases may seem incredibly elusive, even laughable at times. For over a decade I have helped nonprofits with their digital marketing strategy, focusing on social media. What I've found is that when it comes to technology and social media, the hamster wheel never stops, and it's up to the individual nonprofit professional to create a workable plan, or burn out soon after starting.

I find nonprofit professionals excited about all the possibilities and the potential of social media and online marketing, but many of them are overwhelmed with the day to day and feel like their time is not being spent efficiently. They also continually get new tasks added to their plate, all because their supervisor and Board don't understand the real work of social media and the time (and creative brain power) involved.

Hopefully this book will help, but the everyday challenges will undoubtedly remain—as well as the opportunities! Here are my solutions to some of the most common obstacles that nonprofit social media managers face:

1. Information overload and FOMO.

I see information overload and FOMO (fear of missing out) as two sides of the same coin. On the one hand, you know that you can't possibly consume all of those bookmarked articles and saved podcasts, but you fear that you will be missing out on something extra special and helpful if you don't read/listen to/watch all the things.

I once spent half a day unsubscribing to email newsletters. Even so, I don't feel like the time spent got me anywhere. I still have half a dozen blogs to check every day, well-meaning people forwarding interesting articles, plus YouTube video tutorials and podcasts and news alerts and… you get the point.

My solution: Focus on the top two or three topics that are most relevant to your job and to your audience. You do not have to be the go-to resource and topic expert on every single article, trend, or news-story that comes across your desk.

Dedicate some time in your daily routine to look at relevant news and blogs in order to stay current (and to feed the social media content machine). However, make sure that you don't waste your most creative, high energy part of your day doing this. Clicking on links and skimming blog posts can sap your creativity and enthusiasm for other more important projects.

A good way to manage the information fire hose is to filter all of those non-urgent email newsletters into a tab called News, which you can check during a scheduled time in the day. Set an egg timer for 10-15 minutes to review these news sites, and no matter where you are when it goes off, close the browser or save for later.

2. The internet rabbit hole.

Have you ever taken five minutes out of your morning to check Facebook, clicked on an article, then clicked on another article from that article, then all of a sudden you have 50 Chrome tabs open? And it's an hour later and you don't even remember what you were doing in the first place?

My solution: Use the Pomodoro Technique. This is by far the best piece of productivity advice I have ever received. Using a free service like MyTomatoes.com, track where your social media time goes and set concrete parameters. (For a great book on this productivity hack, read *The Pomodoro Technique: The Acclaimed Time-Management System That Has Transformed How We Work* by Francesco Cirillo.)

Keep a regimented, rigorous Pomodoro schedule when it comes to checking your social media accounts. If your only job is to monitor emergency and urgent conversations around your industry and your organization, then by all means keep those tabs open. If your job requires you to complete other non-social-media tasks (and if you work at a nonprofit, I am sure that it does), schedule dedicated time in your calendar to focus solely on checking social media.

I also create special tabs within my email to filter all notifications so that they do not disrupt my email inbox and send me off onto a social media goose chase. Facebook, Twitter, Pinterest and the like get their own folders, and I schedule time in my calendar to monitor these networks one by one, replying to mentions and monitoring followed hashtags.

3. Drowning in social media notifications.

Who doesn't feel like they are drowning in notifications these days? Social media managers are a resilient bunch, because not only do we have to manage our personal social networks, we have to stay on top of our organization's platforms.

My solution: You can choose to schedule your day in defense mode or offense mode. Are you writing a blog post, shooting a video, creating a great Instagram post? That's offense mode, and requires some uninterrupted creativity time.

Response mode refers to the scheduled times of the day (think Pomodoro technique) when you check each platform and respond to questions and comments. If you work well with your mobile apps pinging all day and your laptop buzzing, continue with that structure. If not, segment your time spent on each platform into bigger, dedicated chunks and turn the notifications off the rest of the time.

4. Fire-fighting.

Do you constantly bounce from project to project, fire to fire all day long? Is there no time for strategic planning or big picture thinking? If you feel like you are spending entire days on minutiae and not getting anywhere, consider outsourcing. I had a client who would spend half a day formatting a blog post for WordPress and then another half a day promoting the post to the organization's social media channels. She was also in charge of fundraising for the organization, event planning and all the other marketing initiatives.

We convinced her board to allot her a small budget for a virtual assistant and an intern who ended up saving her hours of WordPress and graphic design work, which she then dedicated to starting a successful major gifts and annual fundraising program. You can also get small tasks done on sites like Fiverr and Intern.org—truly on a shoestring.

Nonprofit Social Media Blueprint Activity: Write down one idea that you will implement in order to stay productive and focused doing this work.

Conclusion

"Social media and technology are not agents of change. They are just tools. We, the connected people, are the agents of change."
—Jean R Lanoue

The most important piece of advice I can give to a busy, stressed out nonprofit social media manager is not to beat yourself up if a few tweets go unanswered, a blog post is a day late, or a Facebook post has a formatting error. Things can be edited and cleaned up. Tomorrow is another day.

Social media and nonprofit marketing work is important—but the work of community building, raising awareness, and showcasing your impact is never fully done, and that's ok.

The future cannot be automated. People are, and will continue to be, motivated by people and not technology. If you give people the information they need, they will take it and run with it on your behalf. Provide them with guidance, clear steps, compelling stories, helpful information—but let them take your message into their own hands. Give them empowerment and ownership of your vision.

In social media, it truly is a game of you get what you give. If you are just showing up to solicit, to push out a promotion, to post and leave—you will not get the results you seek nor the achievements that your cause deserves.

For nonprofit social media managers, the constant challenge is making it easier for your audience and customers to engage with you on their terms—when and where they want to. This is vital to understand—it's not about us and where we want to interact; it's not about what's convenient for us. It's all about our community and their preferences. Without them, we are nothing.

You can't purchase an active online community. You can buy email lists, fans, followers—but not genuine participation and affinity.

Building your movement and mobilizing your community on social media requires skill, patience, and strategic effort, but should never be seen as a waste of time. You've got this.

Send me an email at julia@jcsocialmarketing.com with questions about this book, and be sure to check out all of the tools, tech, and nonprofit examples mentioned in this book at www.jcsocialmarketing.com/socialmediabook

Endnotes

Introduction

Godin, Seth. 2007. "How to be remarkable." The Guardian https://www.theguardian.com/money/2007/jan/06/careers. work5#article_continue

PicLoco, Social Media Manager Perception vs. Fact Meme. https://www.picloco.com/perception-vs-fact/loco/ej/

Brooks, Jeff. 2018. "Saying 'we exist' is not fundraising." Future Fundraising Now. https://www.futurefundraisingnow.com/future-fundraising/2018/12/saying-we-exist-is-not-fundraising.html

Wu, Tim. 2016. *The Attention Merchants: The Epic Scramble to Get Inside Our Heads*. Knopf Publishing.

Andrea, Harris. 2019. "The Human Brain is Loaded Daily with 34 GB of Information." https://www.tech21century.com/the-human-brain-is-loaded-daily-with-34-gb-of-information/

Kietzmann, J.H., Hermkens, K., McCarthy, I.P. and Silvestre, B.S. 2011. "Social media? Get serious! Understanding the functional building blocks of social media." *Business Horizons*. http://summit.sfu.ca/item/18103

Tufekci, Zeynep. 2017. *Twitter and Tear Gas: The Power and Fragility of Networked Protest*. Yale University Press.

Godin, Seth. 2018. *This Is Marketing: You Can't Be Seen Until You Learn to See.* Penguin Publishing Group, a division of Penguin Random House LLC.

Dimock, Michael. 2018. "Our expanded focus on trust, facts and the state of democracy." Pew Research Center. https://www. pewresearch.org/2018/04/26/our-expanded-focus-on-trust-facts-and-the-state-of-democracy/

The 2019 Edelman Trust Barometer, https://www.edelman.com/trust-barometer

Chapter 1–Setting Clear Goals

Godin, Seth. 2018. *This Is Marketing: You Can't Be Seen Until You Learn to See.* Penguin Publishing Group, a division of Penguin Random House LLC.

Chapter 2 –Audience Identification

Levesque, Ryan. 2015. *Ask: The Counterintuitive Online Method to Discover Exactly What Your Customers Want to Buy...Create a Mass of Raving Fans...and Take Any Business to the Next Level.* Dunham Books.

Pew Research Center, 2018 Social Media Use Report. https://www. pewinternet.org/2018/03/01/social-media-use-in-2018/

Chapter 3–A Message that Attracts

Planned Parenthood manifesto, https://www.unstoppablenow.org/manifesto/

Greenpeace Detox Fashion Manifesto, http://www.greenpeace.org/eastasia/campaigns/toxics/get-involved/sign-detox-fashion-manifesto/

Chapter 5–Picking Platforms

Snapchat Business, [US] Apposphere: How the Apps You Use Impact Your Daily Life and Emotions. https://forbusiness.

snapchat.com/blog/apposphere-how-the-apps-you-use-impact-your-daily-life-and-emotions

Shepherd, Brittany. 2018. "The IRS Explains Its Instagram Strategy—and Promises It Won't Get on Any Dating Apps." The Washingtonian. https://www.washingtonian.com/2018/12/04/irs-instagram-strategy/

IRS on Instagram, http://www.instagram.com/irsnews

Pew Research Center, 2018 Social Media Use Report. https://www.pewinternet.org/2018/03/01/social-media-use-in-2018/

Chapter 7—6 Pillars

Nielsen, Jakob. 2006. "The 90-9-1 Rule for Participation Inequality in Social Media and Online Communities." https://www.nngroup.com/articles/participation-inequality/

Plan International UK, The Ring: Why It Matters campaign, https://plan-uk.org/act-for-girls/about-because-i-am-a-girl/how-were-ending-child-marriage/the-ring-campaign-why-it

Berkes, Howard and Grabell, Michael. 2015. "How Much Is Your Arm Worth? Depends On Where You Work." *ProPublica*. https://www.propublica.org/article/how-much-is-your-arm-worth-depends-where-you-work

Speta, Mary. 2018. "That time I almost died in Honduras." Amirah, Inc. blog. https://www.amirahinc.org/single-post/2018/10/16/That-time-I-almost-died-in-Honduras?cat=3

Heath, Chip and Heath, Dan. 2007. Made to Stick: Why Some Ideas Survive and Others Die. Random House.

PETA on Facebook, https://www.facebook.com/watch/?v=10155296501394586

ASPCA advertisement featuring Sarah McLachlan, https://youtu.be/9gspElv1yvc

First Descents on YouTube, https://youtu.be/xpB9Bvd42hk

Everyday WaterAid 360 video campaign, https://www.youtube.
com/playlist?list=PLc-oawSTlDS3D42IJ03Fpi26Vi14bsbHg

"Beginning"—A Pencils of Promise Virtual Reality Film, https://
youtu.be/SelvUz8Zr3k

VR Sanctuary Experience, Best Friends Animal Society, https://
bestfriends.org/vr-sanctuary-experience

Chapter 8—Pillar 2

The Rainforest Alliance, "Follow the Frog", https://www.youtube.
com/watch?v=3iIkOi3srLo

Nirvan Mullick, "Caine's Arcade", https://www.youtube.com/
watch?v=faIFNkdq96U&t=10s

Invisible Children, "Kony 2012", https://www.youtube.com/
watch?v=Y4MnpzG5Sqc

Zaltman, Gerald. 2003. "How Customers Think: Essential Insights
into the Mind of the Market." Harvard Business School Press.

The Intercept, "A Message from the Future With Alexandria
Ocasio-Cortez." https://youtu.be/d9uTH0iprVQ

Greenpeace Story & Content Guide, https://storytelling.greenpeace.
org/

UNICEF on Facebook, https://www.facebook.com/unicef/photos/a.
10150563250124002/10152593826129002/?type=3&theater

The Greater Boston Foodbank on Facebook, https://www.facebook.
com/watch/?v=10155182474216730

Feeding America, "Real Stories of Hunger: Emily", https://www.
youtube.com/watch?time_continue=1&v=NQuz1qkEF8k

Malek, Alia. 2019. "Moving Beyond the Label of 'War Refugee'",
https://www.nytimes.com/2019/05/17/magazine/syria-war-
refugees-europe.html

Feeding America on Instagram, https://www.instagram.com/p/
Bm1Cexsh4nW/

Singing Hope for Communities, "The Kibera School for Girls—I Know I Can, https://www.youtube.com/watch?v=Z4_ZCIgEAd4

Chapter 9–Pillar 3

READ Global, "Meet Chuna: Empowering women in rural Nepal—a READ Global video", https://www.youtube.com/watch?time_continue=19&v=EN19au1tpsU

Rise Academy, "Mia", https://vimeo.com/30161480

Girls Who Code Annual Report 2017, https://girlswhocode.com/2017report/

Campbell, Julia. 2015. "5 Great Nonprofit Infographics to Learn From." https://jcsocialmarketing.com/2014/03/5-great-nonprofit-infographics-learn/

European Parkinson's Disease Association and Parkinson's UK, #UniteForParkinsons campaign, https://uniteforparkinsons.org/

Best Buddies on Instagram, https://www.instagram.com/p/BmYfqfSgGQb/

CHOICE Humanitarian on Facebook, https://www.facebook.com/CHOICEorg/photos/a.201628623272352/1635186369916563/?type=3&theater

Rosie's Place on Instagram, https://www.instagram.com/p/BtRch3zj8Sy/

St. Baldricks Foundation on Facebook, https://www.facebook.com/StBaldricksFoundation/posts/10150867505459978:0

Plummer Youth Promise, https://plummeryouthpromise.org/

Chapter 10–Pillar 4

A Mighty Girl Holiday Gift Guide, https://www.amightygirl.com/holiday-guide

Amirah, Inc. gift guide on Instagram, https://www.instagram.com/p/BrDCvcxhfUv/

American Red Cross on Facebook, https://www.facebook.com/
redcross/photos/a.77178595070/10152576010185071/?type=3
&theater

Our Health California on YouTube, https://www.youtube.com/
channel/UCMYxoswiF4FrW_96P_mA86A

National Aphasia Association, https://www.aphasia.org/

Morning Edition, NPR. 2017. "Sweet, Sweet Little Ramona." https://
www.npr.org/2017/10/04/555520535/sweet-sweet-little-ramona

Susan G. Komen Florida on Instagram, https://www.instagram.com/
stories/komenflorida/

Edwards, Latoya. 2019. Channel 10 Boston, "Girls Inc. and Hearts
on Fire". https://www.nbcboston.com/multimedia/this-is-new-
england-girls-inc-of-lynn-511248302.html?fbclid=IwAR2Hiy2gC
HNhe6ChBcbnB0fj7rgKaYdU89Yj1Eju0LwPL1Uw1VSkYca-_sc

Girls Scouts is #ForEVERYGirl campaign, https://www.indiegogo.
com/projects/girl-scouts-is-foreverygirl#/

Chapter 11—Pillar 5

Ami Musa on Pinterest, https://www.pinterest.com/AmiMusa/pins/

Be Real Campaign website, https://www.berealcampaign.co.uk/
stories

Amirah, Inc. on Facebook, https://www.facebook.com/AmirahInc/
posts/2263123930392437

REACH Beyond Domestic Violence on Facebook, https://www.
facebook.com/reachma/posts/1989544287821376

Edutopia on Instagram, https://www.instagram.com/edutopia/

Caregiver Action Network Social Media Hub, https://
caregiveraction.org/resources/caregiver-social-media-hub

Best Friends Animal Society on Facebook, https://www.facebook.
com/bestfriendsanimalsociety/videos/10154256098651425/

Campbell, Julia. 2017. "Ways Your Nonprofit Can Use Live-
Streaming Video for Better Storytelling." https://trust.guidestar.

org/8-ways-your-nonprofit-can-use-live-streaming-video-for-better-storytelling

MET Museum on Facebook, https://www.facebook.com/pg/metmuseum/videos/

No Kid Hungry on Twitter, https://twitter.com/nokidhungry/status/1067463415319298049

Chapter 12–Pillar 6

Van der Linden, Dr. Dander. 2017. "The nature of viral altruism and how to make it stick." *Nature Human Behaviour.* https://www.nature.com/articles/s41562-016-0041

Planned Parenthood of Illinois Action social media toolkit, https://www.plannedparenthoodaction.org/planned-parenthood-illinois-action/take-action

Vie, Stephanie. 2014. "In defense of 'slacktivism': The Human Rights Campaign Facebook logo as digital activism." *First Monday.* https://firstmonday.org/article/view/4961/3868%20for%20details#author

The Washington Trails Association Hike Finder Map, https://www.wta.org/go-outside/map

The Montana Wilderness Association Wilderness Walks, https://wildmontana.org/discover-the-wild/wilderness-walks

Mind on Instagram, https://www.instagram.com/mindcharity/

WordSwag mobile app, http://wordswag.co/

Canva for Nonprofits, https://about.canva.com/canva-for-nonprofits/

Imgflip, https://imgflip.com/memegenerator

Naperville Area Humane Society on Facebook, https://www.facebook.com/naperhumane/posts/10157436878729665

HubSpot, https://www.hubspot.com/

HootSuite, https://hootsuite.com/

Chapter 13—How to Repurpose Existing Content

Magisto app, https://www.magisto.com/

Animoto app, https://animoto.com/

Storeo app, https://apps.apple.com/us/app/storeo-stories-maker/
   id1207906248

CutStory for Instagram Stories app, https://apps.apple.com/us/app/
   cutstory-for-instagram-stories/id917630934

SlideShare, https://www.slideshare.net/

Malaria No More on Pinterest, https://www.pinterest.com/
   pin/483855553688754201/

DoSomething.org on Instagram, https://www.instagram.com/
   stories/dosomething/

Canva for Nonprofits, https://about.canva.com/canva-for-nonprofits/

Adobe Spark, https://spark.adobe.com/

Visme, https://www.visme.co/

Lucidpress, https://www.lucidpress.com/

The Chronicle of Philanthropy, https://www.philanthropy.com/

NonProfit PRO, https://www.nonprofitpro.com/

Bloomerang, https://bloomerang.co/

NeonCRM, https://www.neoncrm.com/

Classy, https://www.classy.org/

CauseVox, https://www.causevox.com/

Nonprofit Technology Network (NTEN), https://www.nten.org/

Wild Apricot, https://www.wildapricot.com/

Google Hangout, https://tools.google.com/dlpage/hangoutplugin

Facebook Live, https://live.fb.com/

Instagram Live, https://help.instagram.com/292478487812558

Chapter 14—How to Curate Content

HootSuite, https://hootsuite.com/

Buffer, https://buffer.com

Meltwater, https://www.meltwater.com/

Mention.com, https://mention.com/en/

Attentive.ly, https://attentive.ly/

Google Alerts, https://www.google.com/alerts

Scoop.it, https://www.scoop.it/

List.ly, https://list.ly/

Chapter 15—How to Address Challenges

Uplift Repeal Training: Persuasive Conversations. https://www.
crowdcast.io/e/lqn8ums7/register

Craver, Roger. 2017. "Storytelling in the Digital Age." http://agitator.
thedonorvoice.com/storytelling-in-the-digital-age/

AEIOU Foundation on YouTube, https://youtu.be/NJFKJes0_zs

Chapter 16—Slacktivists

Gladwell, Malcom. 2010. "Small Change: Why the revolution will
not be tweeted." *The New Yorker*. https://www.newyorker.com/
magazine/2010/10/04/small-change-malcolm-gladwell

Khazan, Olga. 2013. "UNICEF Tells Slacktivists: Give Money, Not
Facebook Likes." *The Atlantic*. https://www.theatlantic.com/
international/archive/2013/04/unicef-tells-slacktivists-give-
money-not-facebook-likes/275429/

Chapter 17—Monthly Social Media Calendar

Zephoria.com, The Top 20 Valuable Facebook Statistics—Updated
July 2019. https://zephoria.com/top-15-valuable-facebook-
statistics/

Wilco Forest Preserve #BatWeek campaign, https://blog.
adobespark.com/2016/11/29/non-profit-content-marketing-
ideas-15-things-to-share-on-social-media-to-support-a-cause/

Chapter 18—How to Amplify Your Message

Gottlieb, Hildy. 2015. "Building Movements, Not Organizations." *Stanford Social Innovation Review*. https://ssir.org/articles/entry/building_movements_not_organizations

Le, Vu. 2019. "OMG, can we please stop saying 'there's only so much funding to go around'?!" *Nonprofit AF*. https://nonprofitaf.com/2018/11/omg-can-we-please-stop-saying-theres-only-so-much-funding-to-go-around/

#MarchForOurLives movement, https://en.wikipedia.org/wiki/March_for_Our_Lives

#KeepFamiliesTogether movement on Twitter, https://twitter.com/hashtag/keepfamiliestogether

#Overcorrection campaign on Twitter, https://twitter.com/propublica/status/1121046098741747712

#GivingTuesday, https://twitter.com/hashtag/keepfamiliestogether

Silberman, Michael. 2018. "Four ways nonprofits are learning from March for Our Lives, Keep Families Together and a new wave of people-powered action." *MobLab*. https://mobilisationlab.org/four-ways-nonprofits-learn-marchforourlives/

Chapter 19—Social Media Ambassadors

Baer, Jay. 2014. "The 8 Things Online Influencers Can Do For You." https://www.slideshare.net/jaybaer/8-things-online-influencers-can-do-for-you/3-92of_global_consumers_trustUGC_and

Greenpeace Social Media Hive, https://www.greenpeace.org/usa/join-the-social-media-hive/

State College of Florida Foundation Social Media Ambassador program, https://www.scf-foundation.org/social-media-ambassadors/

Watts of Love Social Media Ambassador program, https://www.wattsoflove.org/new-index#social-media

The Massachusetts Conference for Women Social Media Street Team, https://www.maconferenceforwomen.org/conference/social-media/

Susan G. Komen Florida video campaign with CauseVid, https://app.causevid.com/volunteerModule/bc2b2b44-ccb0-11e8-a8d5-f2801f1b9fd1

Susan G. Komen Florida Social Media Ambassador program, https://komenflorida.org/social-media-ambassador/

Crossroad Child & Family Services on Facebook, https://www.facebook.com/crossroad.cares/posts/10156033372148896

The National Osteoporosis Foundation Brand Ambassador program, https://www.nof.org/about-us/building-awareness/

Chapter 20—Social Media Toolkit

Hanley, Ryan. 2015. "7 Ways to Use Facebook native Video to Better Connect With Your Fans. " *Social Media Examiner*. https://www.socialmediaexaminer.com/facebook-native-video/

Denver Rescue Mission Stories of Changed Lives, https://denverrescuemission.org/what-we-do/stories-of-change/

Road Scholar blog, "What the Heck is Instagram? Inside the App." https://discussion.roadscholar.org/b/blog/posts/what-the-heck-is-instagram-inside-the-app

Chapter 21—Connect with Influencers

Blackbaud and Small Act infographic, A Meet & Greet With Your Favorite Social Archetypes. https://cdn1.hubspot.com/hub/297253/file-314966579.png?__hstc=169971071.ac26446ad8da2e65e6de3bf200acf7ff.1412710032462.1412710032462.1412710032462.1&__hssc=169971071.1.1412710032462&__hsfp=4269358367

Nonprofit Podcasts and Video Shows, bit.ly/nonprofitpodcasts

Chapter 23—How to Measure Success

Kanter, Beth. 2012. "Say So What To Your Data Three Times."
http://www.bethkanter.org/sowhat/

Chapter 24—Productivity

The Pomodoro Technique, https://francescocirillo.com/pages/
pomodoro-technique

MyTomatoes.com

Dichter, Sasha. 2008. "In Defense of Raising Money: a Manifesto
for NonProfit CEOs." https://sashadichter.files.wordpress.
com/2008/10/manifesto-in-defense-of-raising-money_sasha1.pdf

Made in the USA
Las Vegas, NV
06 June 2021

24295442R00164